Distant Cousins:
The Caribbean-Latin American
Relationship

Distant Cousins

The Caribbean-Latin American Relationship

Edited by
Anthony T. Bryan and Andrés Serbin

The mission of the North-South Center is to promote better relations and serve as a catalyst for change among the United States, Canada, and the nations of Latin America and the Caribbean by advancing knowledge and understanding of the major political, social, economic, and cultural issues affecting the nations and peoples of the Western Hemisphere.

© 1996 by the University of Miami. Published by the North-South Center Press, University of Miami, and distributed by Lynne Rienner Publishers, Inc., 1800 30th Street, Suite 314, Boulder, CO 80301-1026. All rights reserved under International and Pan-American Conventions. No portion of the contents may be reproduced or transmitted in any form, or by any means, including photocopying, recording, or any information storage retrieval system, without prior permission in writing from the publisher. All copyright inquiries should be addressed to the North-South Center Press, University of Miami, P.O. Box 248205, Coral Gables, Florida 33124-3027.

To order or to return books, contact Lynne Rienner Publishers, Inc., 1800 30th Street, Suite 314, Boulder, CO 80301-1026, 303-444-6684, fax 303-444-0824.

Library of Congress Cataloging-in-Publication Data
Distant cousins: the Caribbean-Latin American relationship / edited
    by Anthony T. Bryan and Andrés Serbin.
        p. cm.
    Includes bibliographical references and index.
    ISBN 1-57454-003-3 (alk. paper: pbk.)
        1. Latin America—Relations—West Indies, British. 2. West
Indies, British—Relations—Latin America. I. Bryan, Anthony t.
II. Serbin, Andrés.
F1416.W47D5 1996
303.4'82729—dc20   96-28718
                                                              CIP

ISBN-1-57454-003-3

Printed in the United States of America, TS/DM

00 99 98 97 96 8 7 6 5 4 3 2 1

Contents

Preface and Acknowledgments

Some 20 years ago, the co-editors of this volume, Anthony T. Bryan and Andrés Serbin, began to develop a strong academic interest in the study of relations between the English-speaking states of the Caribbean and the countries of Latin America — primarily the sociological, political, and cultural architecture of the relationship. This relationship is the topic of this collection of essays.

The Caribbean region and Latin America are part of the same matrix. When the definition of the Caribbean is taken at its widest, it includes the insular Caribbean, the northern littoral states of South America, Central America, and the Caribbean coast of Mexico. The English-speaking (or Commonwealth) Caribbean countries comprise a very small segment of the hemisphere, if measured in terms of land and population, size, economic resources, and security capabilities. Yet interaction and cooperation between these states and their larger Latin American neighbors have not been as strong nor as sustained over time as might have been expected. Even cultural exchange, technical and economic cooperation, and trade have not evolved automatically from geographic proximity. In the past, the respective colonial policies of exclusive vertical relations with European states had set the pattern and the legacy. As the contributors to this volume stress, historical, cultural, and linguistic differences also have colored the mutual perceptions of the peoples of both groups of countries. It is only during the past 30 years that there has been some progressive alteration of this circumstance.

In this work, several dimensions of the Caribbean-Latin American relationship are explored. There is a bias toward the relations of the islands with the Latin American mainland countries that border on the Caribbean Sea. In this interdisciplinary sampling, the synergies of the relationship are explored by Andrés Serbin (politics), Glenn Sankatsing (culture and education), Francine Jácome (national identity and race), Lulú Giménez Saldivia (literature), Christopher R. Thomas (hemispheric cooperation), Henry S. Gill (the Association of Caribbean States), and Anthony T. Bryan (future dynamics).

The contributors represent a mix of Latin American and Caribbean scholars, and their views vary widely. The editors have chosen not to impose any artificial consensus. They leave it to the readers to improve their own understanding of the issues by exploring the different analyses. We affirm, however, that the future of the wider Caribbean region depends on a rejection of the old prejudices that separate the region's peoples and on the pursuit of further initiatives that transcend geographical and national boundaries.

The book is a product of the Caribbean Program at the North-South Center. The research was done as a joint project by the Venezuelan Institute of Social and Political Studies (INVESP) and the Institute of International Relations of the University of the West Indies, Trinidad, and coordinated by Andrés Serbin and Anthony T. Bryan. The editors wish to acknowledge the financial support provided by the Ford Foundation and the Department of Cultural Affairs of the Organization of American States.

The final product represents a collective effort on the part of the authors and the editors. But it could not have been published without the support and cooperation of a number of other individuals at the North-South Center. Our thanks to Ambassador Ambler H. Moss, Jr., director; Dr. Robin Rosenberg, deputy director; Jeffrey Stark, director of research and studies; Kathleen Hamman, editorial director of the North-South Center Press; Mary M. Mapes, publications director; Susan K. Holler, associate publications director; and Jayne M. Weisblatt, senior editor.

Anthony T. Bryan and Andrés Serbin

Contributors

Bryan, Anthony T. Director of the Caribbean Program, North-South Center, University of Miami. Former Director of the Institute of International Relations and Professor of International Relations at the University of the West Indies, Trinidad, and Senior Associate, Carnegie Endowment for International Peace, Washington, D.C.

Gill, Henry S. International Relations Consultant based in Trinidad and Tobago. Former Deputy Permanent Secretary of the Latin American Economic System (Caracas) and Mellon Visiting Professor at Florida International University.

Giménez Saldivia, Lulú. Research Fellow, Centro de Estudios Latinoamericanos Rómulo Gallegos (CELARG), Caracas.

Jácome, Francine. Professor, Escuela de Estudios Internacionales de la Universidad Central de Venzuela and Director of the Instituto Venezolano de Estudios Sociales y Políticos (INVESP), Caracas.

Sankatsing, Glenn. Research Associate, Instituto Venezolano de Estudios Sociales y Políticos (INVESP), Caracas, and former Director of the Institute of Economic and Social Research, University of Suriname.

Serbin, Andrés. Special Adviser to the Latin American Economic System (SELA). Professor, Escuelas de Sociología y de Relaciones Internacionales de la Universidad Central de Venezuela, and President of the Instituto Venezolano de Estudios Sociales y Políticos (INVESP), Caracas.

Thomas, Christopher R. Assistant Secretary-General, Organization of American States, Washington, D.C. Senior Diplomat and former Permanent Secretary of the Ministry of External Relations of Trinidad and Tobago. Former Ambassador of Trinidad and Tobago to Venezuela and Lecturer, Institute of International Relations, University of the West Indies, Trinidad.

Chapter One

Should Latin America Be Interested in the Caribbean? A Review of the Political Relationship

Andrés Serbin

Introduction

The links between Caribbean and Latin American countries are primarily relations between the independent English-speaking Caribbean states and the Latin American circum-Caribbean continental nations. There are exceptions to this pattern. Cuba and the Dominican Republic historically have tended to perceive themselves, and to be perceived by the non-Hispanic Caribbean, as part of Latin America. Haiti is regarded by Spanish-speaking countries as part of Latin America because of its historical and cultural links with France and by the non-Hispanic states as part of the Caribbean because of its African legacy. Puerto Rico has an ambiguous status as a Spanish-speaking Caribbean country, while it is also an associated state of the United States. Additionally, several insular Caribbean states view Mexico, Colombia, and Venezuela (and sometimes Brazil) as part of Latin America with no consistent links to the insular Caribbean. Also, the French Departments d'Outremer (DOM) and the Dutch territories of Aruba, Curaçao, Bonaire, Saba, St. Eustatius, and St. Maarten, plus the associated states of the United Kingdom (Anguilla, Bermuda, Cayman Islands, Turks and Caicos, Montserrat, and British Virgin Islands), are seen as part of the European presence in the region (Beltrán and Serbin 1992).

Nurtured by linguistic diversity, ethnic heterogeneity, and cultural and political fragmentation that historically have distinguished the region, multiple definitions of the Caribbean have proliferated since the 1960s (Knight and Palmer 1989, Serbin 1991a and 1993a). Within this context, Latin American-Caribbean relations have been marked by the imprint of colonial legacies reflected in the current cultural, ethnic, and linguistic barriers; the persistence of border disputes; and the evident economic differences in size,

1

development stages, and economic potential. This complex set of factors has contributed to the development of strongly rooted negative perceptions and stereotypes on all sides, which have influenced not only popular attitudes but also the formal relations among governments and states of the English-speaking Caribbean and of Latin America (Serbin 1985, 1987, 1991b, 1993a).

Since the 1960s, when many of the English-speaking Caribbean states became politically independent, relations with Latin American countries often have been characterized by mutual mistrust and suspicion, frequently bolstered by little knowledge or total ignorance of each other (Serbin and Bryan 1990).

This general pattern of relations is not a fixed one. It has evolved since the 1960s through four different stages, broadly associated with the distinctive geopolitical traits of each of the four decades of existing relations.

The 1960s: Mistrust and Antagonism

The first stage, generally associated with the establishment of formal diplomatic relations between the two groups of countries, was marked by the colonial legacy of mutual distrust and suspicion, in a very particular regional context. This context was characterized at the time by the persistent presence of the European powers, the Cold War and its impact on the region, and the subsequent sequels of U.S. intervention and Organization of American States (OAS) blockage and isolation of Cuba. One of the heights of U.S. strategic concern about the Caribbean was in the period when, for the first time, the Caribbean began to be perceived as a specific subregion in the hemispheric context with its own particular geopolitical dynamics (Serbin 1989a).

The best illustration of the difficult relations between the recently independent non-Hispanic Caribbean states and the Latin American countries was in the early 1960s, when Trinidad and Tobago and Jamaica applied to become members of the Organization of American States (OAS) despite the automatic exclusion of Guyana because of its pending border dispute with Venezuela. The governments of both countries considered this an important step toward gaining access to Inter-American Development Bank (IDB) loans, which at this time were still tied to OAS membership, even if they resented the "Ibero American" orientation conferred upon the organization by the Latin American governments (Serbin 1993a).

Some of the Latin American representatives at the OAS deferred the acceptance of Trinidad and Tobago's and Jamaica's applications for more than one year. The reasons behind this delay were related to the generalized Latin American perception that the inclusion of former British colonies in the organization might allow the United Kingdom to exercise a degree of influence over inter-American affairs and that the English-speaking Caribbean countries could eventually break the regional isolation imposed on Cuba (Bryan 1979, Ince 1980, Serbin 1985). From the Latin American perspective, both suspicions proved to be true, even if their effects were delayed. In 1972, four of the English-speaking Caribbean governments formally established diplomatic relations with Cuba before the breaking by other Latin American countries of the OAS isolation policy imposed on the island (Maingot 1983). Ten years later, all of the former British territories (with the exception of Grenada, which at this time was closely associated with Cuba) aligned themselves with the British position during the Malvinas/Falkland crisis (Ely 1983).

The 1970s: Rapprochement and "Third Worldism"

The 1970s were characterized by a first attempt to change this initial pattern of relations. The new international and regional context was characterized by the dramatic increase in the price of oil and other raw materials on the international market, which benefited some Caribbean and Latin American countries. This situation stimulated a growing autonomy in the foreign affairs of those economically fortunate states. The promotion of a "Third World" discourse and atmosphere further emphasized South-South cooperation and the establishment of a new international economic order. Within this context, the regional "middle powers," such as Mexico, Colombia, Venezuela, and Cuba, increased their involvement in the Caribbean Basin in search of a different approach to the geostrategic interests promoted by the United States. Some of the more developed English-speaking Caribbean countries saw the opportunity to diversify their regional links (Paget and Stone 1983, Grabendorff 1984).

The best illustration of this explicit attempt to break the established pattern of relations between the two groups of countries was the creation in 1975 of the Latin American Economic System (SELA), initiated by Prime Minister Michael Manley of Jamaica and Presidents Luis Echeverría of Mexico and Carlos Andrés Pérez of Venezuela. This initiative made use of existing political links to establish the first bridges between Latin America and the Caribbean (including Cuba), and it excluded the United States. Other initiatives, such as the creation of a regional maritime transport network (NAMUCAR) and the establishment of bauxite and banana producers' associations, were also significant attempts in this direction (Serbin 1993a).

Simultaneously, Venezuela, Mexico, and Colombia joined the Caribbean Development Bank (CDB) as donors; Cuba launched a specific policy toward the non-Hispanic Caribbean, stressing its Afro-Latin identity; and Venezuela and Mexico took a first step in establishing the San José Pact of oil assistance to the Caribbean Basin. Initiatives by Mexico, Venezuela, and Colombia were clearly intended to break their isolation from the rest of Latin

America (due to the proliferation of military regimes in the Southern Cone) and to develop new alliances and diplomatic convergences in the hemisphere, increasing their autonomy from the United States (Maira 1983).

However, despite the strong "Third World" rhetoric of the 1970s, some of the English-speaking governments were reluctant to follow this path of rapprochement and did not join in the attempts to establish closer links with Latin America. Instead, they stressed a restrained view of the Caribbean and its interests. The government of Eric Williams in Trinidad and Tobago exemplified this position and the reluctance of some English-speaking states to embark on the development of stronger ties with Latin American countries (Maingot 1984, Heine and Manigat 1988, Braveboy-Wagner 1989). A recurrent topic in this atmosphere was the reference to the "subhegemonic" or "subimperialist" objectives of some of the Latin American governments and, particularly, of Venezuela in the region (Manigat 1983).

The 1980s: External Debt and New Priorities

The third stage of Latin American-Caribbean relations developed in the 1980s and was characterized by a retreat to the traditional pattern of mistrust and indifference. The impact of the external debt crisis and the deepening of the domestic economic crises in the countries of the region at this stage were linked to the resurgence of the Cold War in the Caribbean Basin. The intensification of the Central American political crisis and of the more active U.S. regional policy promoted by the Reagan administration (Greene and Scowcroft 1984) characterized this period.[1]

After the early 1980s, the "Third World" rhetoric of the 1970s gradually waned, replaced by an increasing awareness of the domestic problems faced by the Caribbean governments and their linkages with the external debt crisis. Most governments in the region established new priorities in their foreign policies, creating the conditions for a new round of increasing indifference between the Latin American and English-speaking Caribbean countries. Perhaps the only instance of a sustained policy toward the region was the maintenance of a renewed Venezuelan "Caribbean policy," which stressed the importance of cultural and economic cooperation through "shared responsibility" (Serbin 1990).

Two specific geopolitical situations contributed to deepening the existing abyss between both groups of countries in the 1980s. First, the Malvinas/Falkland crisis aligned the Latin American and the Caribbean Common Market and Community (CARICOM) states on opposite sides (Ely 1983). Second, the Grenada invasion was perceived by Latin American countries as a strictly English-speaking issue; even the OAS did not become involved in any significant manner (Heine 1990).

The 1990s: Toward a New Pattern of Relations?

The fourth stage of relations between Latin America and the English-speaking Caribbean began to develop in the late 1980s. Its evolution was clearly marked by the global and hemispheric changes that have characterized the emergence of new issues and priorities in the international and regional agendas. The end of the Cold War implied a lesser strategic importance of the Caribbean Basin for the traditional external actors involved in the region. Moreover, increasing economic globalization and interdependence raised Eastern Europe to a higher foreign policy priority for the United States and the European powers and promoted the consolidation of three economic groups — the European Union (EU), North American Free Trade Agreement (NAFTA), and Japan. This new situation brought about a growing regional concern regarding the eventual marginalization of the Caribbean from the international economic system (Bryan et al. 1990, Rodríguez Beruff et al. 1991, Serbin 1991a and 1992a).

As a reaction, Latin America and the Caribbean have undergone accelerated subregional integration since 1990. Some previous schemes, such as the Andean Group, CARICOM, and the Central American Common Market (CACM), have been revitalized. In addition, new schemes such as the Group of Three (Mexico, Colombia, and Venezuela [G-3]) and MERCOSUR (Argentina, Brazil, Paraguay, and Uruguay [Southern Cone Common Market]) have been created. Bilateral initiatives for trade liberalization and economic cooperation have advanced (Serbin 1993b). These subregional integration processes, accompanied by implementation of structural adjustment policies in most of the countries, emerged before NAFTA and the Enterprise for the Americas Initiative (EAI) were launched by the Bush administration (Weintraub 1991). In the Caribbean Basin, regional actors were especially concerned about the future of preferential economic assistance and cooperation arrangements promoted through the Caribbean Basin Initiative, the Lomé Convention, the Caribbean program, and the advance of the NAFTA negotiations (Gill and Serbin 1993, Gill 1993). In this context, the recommendations of the West Indian Commission, appointed by CARICOM to assess the new international situation and its impact on the region, stressed the need to deepen existing links with Latin America and jointly to promote, under the aegis of the English-speaking Caribbean, the creation of an Association of Caribbean States (ACE) (WIC 1992).

This English-speaking Caribbean initiative was matched by steps taken by the G-3 in the same direction. The G-3 arranged for its members to be incorporated as observers to CARICOM, established nonreciprocal free trade agreements with CARICOM and the Central American states, and accelerated its own trade liberalization process (Serbin 1991b and 1993b).[2] The G-3 members took these steps out of their increasing concern for regional stability at the end of the Cold War, when the external actors began to show a decreasing strategic interest in the Caribbean Basin (Serbin 1993b).

At the same time, similar steps were taken by the CARICOM and Central American countries, as in the February 1992 meeting promoted by President Rafael Callejas of Honduras and Prime Minister Michael Manley of Jamaica. This initiative was hindered by the competition between the two groups of countries regarding preferential access to the European banana market (*Caribbean Insight* 1993a) and a disagreement vis-à-vis their position toward Cuba and the U.S. economic embargo. A similar situation arose between the CARICOM countries and the Dominican Republic, again with regard to the European banana market, despite their common participation in the Lomé Convention.[3] In addition, Cuba is of particular concern for regional Caribbean actors because of its potential economic competitiveness both with the insular Caribbean countries and the continental Latin American states. As part of its attempt to break the increasing isolation imposed by a hostile U.S. policy, Cuba is trying to establish new diplomatic and commercial links with both groups. The establishment of a joint CARICOM-Cuba commission in 1993 and the inclusion of Cuba in the Association of Caribbean States when it was founded in July 1994 were significant steps in this direction.

The main regional groups — the G-3, CARICOM, and the Central American countries — are showing a growing awareness of the need to promote political cooperation and diplomatic coordination through economic cooperation because of the further evolution of NAFTA, relations with the European Union (EU), and the regional security situation. This general trend is reflected in the active diplomatic exchange and interaction currently being promoted by the governments of the Caribbean Basin countries. Increased regional cooperation has led to several collective diplomatic actions with respect to the recent Haitian and Surinamese crises, despite significant differences in terms of foreign policy objectives, priorities, and principles (Serbin 1993b). The establishment of the Association of Caribbean States (ACE) is the best illustration of commitment to regional strength.

The Societal Network and the Process of Regionalism

These regional initiatives taken by the Caribbean Basin governments are matched significantly by increasing links and relations among nongovernmental actors. As a consequence of the growing complexity of contemporary international relations and the emergence of new actors who promote transnational relations, the region is developing a societal network that is building the basis for a new kind of regional consciousness. The Caribbean Basin's political and economic elites are promoting closer relations between Hispanic and non-Hispanic countries. The newly found common ground is market based — associated with structural adjustment policies, trade liberalization initiatives, and a new approach for developing economic liberalization and export-led growth strategies. Simultaneously, societal transnational links are developing gradually, stressing different social and political objectives and distinctive development and social strategies, and overcoming linguistic, ethnic, and cultural differences in the promotion of a new view of the region.

In recent decades, scholars, intellectuals, and academic researchers have established a regional academic network. Universities and research institutes and centers have participated in the activities of the Association of Caribbean Universities and Research Institutes (UNICA) since the late 1960s. A Caribbean Studies Association (CSA) was established in the 1970s, joined by scholars and intellectuals from different linguistic and cultural areas of the Caribbean, including Venezuela, Mexico, and Colombia. In the 1980s, new professional and academic associations emerged, including the Regional Coordination of Social and Economic Research (CRIES) in Nicaragua, which established a specific Caribbean branch with the participation of Jamaican and Dominican researchers; the Working Group of Caribbean International Relations of the Latin American Council of Social Sciences (CLACSO) based in Puerto Rico; and the Association of Caribbean Economists (ACE). Simultaneously, new research centers and Caribbean Studies associations blossomed in the entire region.[4] Most of these institutes and associations are linked to regional organizations and some of them to regional non-governmental organizations (NGOs), promoting joint regional research projects and a growing regional awareness, while at the same time overcoming linguistic, cultural, and ethnic barriers.

In some cases, those organizations are funded and supported by extraregional NGOs; others are strictly local. Overwhelmingly, they are bringing new, relevant issues to the regional agenda. Grass roots and religious organizations, women's action groups and movements, environmental associations, human rights groups, and peace and disarmament movements are developing alternative strategies and involving new actors in a transnational web of regional relations. Most of these movements and groups, even if they emerge from local or national origins, are gradually moving to regional action, often on the basis of strong criticism of the existing economic policies and the promotion of alternative strategies (Lewis 1991, Deere 1990). The Caribbean Council of Churches in the religious and grass roots movement, the Caribbean Association for Feminist Research and Action (CAFRA) among the women's action and research groups, the "Proyecto Paz y Justicia" in Puerto Rico as a promoter of human rights and peace and disarmament movements, and the Caribbean Conservationist Association as an environmental pressure group are some of the most relevant examples of this process.

Various NGOs' views of the region and of the responses to the changing international and domestic environments are, however, not always convergent. Certain of these groups perceive the Caribbean as part of a hemispheric complex in which close relations with Latin America act as a counterbalance to the links with the United States. For others, the view is restricted to the insular Caribbean as a more homogeneous subregion in terms of economic and social commonalities, despite cultural, linguistic, and ethnoracial differences. Nevertheless, most of the groups are contributing to the development of a new regional awareness in a complex and pluralistic framework. This sometimes brings them into conflict with the existing governmental and business-oriented movements or, in other cases, significantly stymies their progress.

Current Trends

The current trend toward an increasing regional awareness has expanded from the restricted political and economic elites linked to diplomatic and business relations or from the academic and intellectual circles concerned about equity, social justice, and human rights to a more complex and diversified societal tendency toward regionalism, promoted by a wide spectrum of social and political actors. What we are witnessing is the emergence of a new pattern of relations between the Latin American and Caribbean countries, where horizontal links (despite the imprint of colonial legacies and contemporary economic and political ties) are multiplying. In this regard, an initiative such as the Association of Caribbean States might acquire new content and dimensions in response to the new and changing international and regional situation, even though it was launched within the framework of foreign policy objectives.

Latin America and the Caribbean's deepening regionalism is manifesting itself through growing linkages and networking that go beyond traditional contacts of migration or cultural identification. This trend seems to be irreversible and may well lead to the development of a Caribbean Basin economic and political bloc and to reinforcement of existing cultural and communications channels through more effective mass media management, educational programs, and interstate and transnational policies and cultural initiatives (Sankatsing 1990, Antonuccio 1993).

Eventually, the protectionist approach of the main economic blocs, the uncertain evolution of the World Trade Organization (WTO), and U.S. concerns for its own domestic economic problems could be decisive external factors in this process. Also, the centripetal force of NAFTA (despite its short-term threats to the Caribbean economies) and the growing rift between the Southern Cone and the Caribbean Basin Latin American countries are hemispheric variables that have to be taken into account.

Endogenous factors such as economic asymmetries and distinctive economic vulnerabilities among the Caribbean Basin countries and the different pace and objectives of the economic adjustment programs and their particular social and political effects on regional security and political stability could hinder the process toward regionalism. Despite these obstacles, the current stage of the relations between the Latin American countries and the English-speaking Caribbean countries gradually is heralding a new pattern of interrelations and a new view of regionalism. These changes are based not only upon traditional government and elite initiatives but also on an increasingly solid ground of societal links involving a complex set of actors, social and political processes, and development strategies.

Given this apparently irreversible trend toward regionalism, one key question remains: From the perspective of Latin American countries, why should Latin America be interested in the Caribbean?

Why Should Latin America Be Interested in the Caribbean?

Even if the picture presented so far demonstrates that there are other actors increasingly involved in the process of regionalism and in setting a new regional agenda, the main initiatives toward rapprochement and cooperation continue to be promoted by the respective governments within the priorities and objectives established for each state's foreign policy. First, we have to underline that the current trend toward regionalism in the Caribbean Basin is not shared by all Latin American states. The main proponents of regionalism are Colombia, Mexico, and Venezuela (the G-3) and Cuba, countries that have traditionally been aware of regional dynamics. Furthermore, even if some Latin American countries are searching for markets in the Caribbean (such as Argentina and Ecuador), they have shown a clear reluctance to include the CARICOM countries in the Rio Group or in other Latin American political coordination forums. At the same time, uncertainty about the evolution and extension of NAFTA is creating the conditions for the emergence of a South American Free Trade Agreement (SAFTA) built around MERCOSUR and the Latin American Integration Association (ALADI), with Brazil assuming a crucial leadership role. Second, if we disaggregate Latin American interests by economic (trade, investment, and technological transfer or cooperation), societal (migration), environmental, political, and security dimensions, even for the four Latin American countries (Colombia, Cuba, Mexico, and Venezuela) that are most involved in the Caribbean, their interests seem to lie primarily in the political and geopolitical spheres.

Notwithstanding the contemporary emphasis on economic issues and trade, the English-speaking Caribbean represents a small market of scarcely six million people. The four involved Latin American countries are interested mainly in the diversification of trade links through export-oriented strategies directed toward more industrialized areas. Mexico's and Venezuela's 1990 exports to the CARICOM countries did not exceed 1 percent and 2.3 percent, respectively, of their total exports; for Venezuela, imports from CARICOM represented scarcely 1.7 percent of total imports in 1990 (Grandguillhome 1990, 119). The "Caribbeanization" of Cuba did not lead to a significant increase in trade with the CARICOM countries, even as a way to avoid the U.S. economic embargo (González 1990, Domínguez 1993).

Additionally, the asymmetries between the Caribbean Basin Latin American countries and the non-Hispanic Caribbean states offer too little room for investment or technological cooperation. The trend in those sectors appears to be from Latin America to the Caribbean, rather than vice versa. In the investment area, Mexico and Venezuela are the most active, while Cuba aspires to become more involved in technological cooperation (Maingot 1992). Similarly, the G-3 initiative of establishing nonreciprocal free trade agreements with Central America and the Caribbean seems to be more a political move than a search for economic advantage (Serbin 1993b).

From the societal perspective, for Latin American countries involved in the Caribbean Basin, concerns about inward or outward migration are more related to their own neighbors (Venezuela and the Colombian migration; Mexico and the Central American migration; Cuban emigration toward the United States) than to the intraregional flows related to the non-Hispanic Caribbean. Similarly, excluding the case of Cuba, even in a scenario of environmental crisis in the Caribbean Sea, the Latin American mainland countries are more concerned with the Amazon Basin (Brazil, Colombia, and Venezuela) or with the North American and Central American environmental border problems (Mexico), where the issues at stake are more clearly identified with North-South differences.

However, Latin American interests in the Caribbean countries seem particularly relevant in the political and geopolitical domains. The political stability of the region is a major concern for those countries, as shown by the preoccupation of the G-3 with the Cuban political transition, the evolution of the Haitian and Surinamese crises, and the drug-trafficking control agreements among Latin American and Caribbean countries. This growing political and security interest is matched by the new relevance of Caribbean Basin affairs to the international agenda of Latin American states, resulting from the hemispheric fragmentation between the G-3 countries and the Southern Cone and the need to balance links with the United States. Furthermore, the alliances and diplomatic convergences with the Caribbean countries offer the additional advantage of contributing to the promotion of collective subre-gional interests and increasing the leverage of Caribbean Basin Latin American countries in international and hemispheric forums such as the Organization of American States (OAS), the Rio Group, and the United Nations.

Even in the framework of this general Latin American approach to the Caribbean, each of the four mentioned Latin American actors pursues different objectives and has different priorities in the political and geopolitical domains. For Mexico, the Caribbean is of secondary importance in its attempts to counterbalance the integration process with North America through low-cost maintenance of Latin American links (González and Chabat 1993). But for Venezuela, the Caribbean still holds a "vital" strategic importance in its subregional policies, particularly in the context of a more restricted foreign policy. For Colombia, the non-Hispanic Caribbean constitutes an appendix of the joint political and economic subregional initiatives undertaken with Venezuela. Finally, for Cuba, the main interlocutors in the attempt to break the isolation imposed by the United States are the Latin American states in general and the G-3 in particular. These countries can also act as a bridge for Cuba in improving and diversifying links with the European Community through forums such as the Ibero-American Summits.[5]

In general, for the Latin American countries, the main reasons to contribute to the established trend toward regionalism in the Caribbean Basin are related to their political and geopolitical concerns both in the Caribbean Basin and in the larger hemisphere. They are conscious that the trends toward fragmentation, because of further subregional integration, could lead to a reappraisal of certain aspects of the political rift between the Southern Cone and the Caribbean Basin Latin American countries that characterized the 1970s.

Finally, if this analysis is correct in general terms, we can foresee in the medium term the gradual increased involvement and influence of the Caribbean Basin Latin American countries in the regionalism process in the area. We can also predict a reaction by the non-Hispanic Caribbean countries once they perceive their diminishing capacity to continue to lead this subregional process, particularly when compared with the group of Central American states of similar size. In this respect, perhaps the current aspirations of the CARICOM countries and Venezuela to take the lead in a potent Association of Caribbean States might just be another oversized mirage in a new international order, where even medium-sized actors find it difficult to reassert themselves.

Notes

1.   One of the best examples of this policy was the launching, in 1983, of the Caribbean Basin Initiative (CBI), which originally was supposed to be supported by Canada, Mexico, Venezuela, and Colombia.

2.   Venezuela went further in this direction, applying in 1991 for full membership in CARICOM.

3. As a consequence, the Dominican Republic is currently trying to establish closer ties with the Central American countries (Lewis 1993).

4.   Centers and associations include the Venezuelan Institute of Social and Political Studies (INVESP) and the Venezuelan Association of Caribbean Studies (AVECA); the Center for Economic Research (CIECA) and the Latin American Social Sciences Faculty (FLACSO) (with a postgraduate course on Caribbean relations) in the Dominican Republic, Cuba, and Venezuela; new research units at the University of the West Indies, including a Working Group on Latin American-Caribbean Relations at the Institute of International Relations in Trinidad; and a recently founded Mexican Association of Caribbean Studies in Mexico.

5.   In this regard, it is important to take into account the Ibero-American links and the aspirations of Spain and the G-3 to play a significant role in the Cuban political transition.

References

Antonuccio, Pedro. 1993. "Medios masivos de comunicación: Proyección regional y conformación de imágenes y estereotipos." In *Diversidad cultural y tensión regional: América Latina y el Caribe,* ed. Francine Jacome. Caracas: INVESP/ Nueva Sociedad.

Beltrán, Luis, and Andrés Serbin, eds. 1992. *El Caribe entre Europa y América.* Caracas: INVESP/Nueva Sociedad.

Braveboy-Wagner, Jacqueline. 1989. *The Caribbean in World Affairs.* Boulder, Colo.: Westview.

Bryan, Anthony, J. Edward Greene, and Timothy M. Shaw, eds. 1990. *Peace, Development and Security in the Caribbean.* London: Macmillan.

Bryan, Anthony. 1979. "Commonwealth Caribbean - Latin American Relations: Emerging Patterns of Cooperation and Conflict." In *Contemporary International Relations in the Caribbean,* ed. Basil Ince. St. Augustine, Fla.: Institute of International Relations.

Deere, Carmen, ed. 1990. *In the Shadow of the Sun. Caribbean Development Alternatives and U.S. Policy.* Boulder, Colo.: Westview/PACCA.

Domínguez, Jorge. 1993. "Cuba in a New World." Unpublished ms.

Ely, Roland. 1983. *Olas de las Malvinas.* Mérida: Libro Azul.

Gill, Henry, and Andrés Serbin. 1993. "El Caribe de habla inglesa y la iniciativa para las Américas." In *América Latina y la iniciativa para las Américas,* ed. Francisco Rojas Aravena. Santiago: FLACSO.

Gill, Henry. 1993. "Defining a Caribbean Position on NAFTA." Paper presented at the 4th Conference of the Association of Caribbean Economists, Curaçao, June 22-25.

González, Guadalupe, and Jorge Chabat. 1993. "Las opciones hemiféricas de México en el nuevo contexto mundial." Paper presented to the 34th Meeting of the International Studies Association, Acapulco, March 23-27.

González, Gerardo. 1990. *El Caribe en la política exterior de Cuba.* Santo Domingo: CIPROS.

Grabendorff, Wolf. 1984. "Las potencias regionales en la crisis centroamericana: Una comparación de las políticas de México, Venezuela, Cuba y Colombia." In *Entre la autonomía y la subordinación. Política exterior de los países latinoamericanos,* eds. Heraldo Muñoz and Joseph Tulchin. Buenos Aires: Grupo Editor Latinoamericano.

Granguillhome, Rogelio. 1990. "Comentarios sobre las relaciones entre México y el Caribe: Aspectos comerciales y financieros." In *El Caribe: Nuestra tercera frontera,* ed. Instituto Matías Romero de Estudios Diplomáticos. Mexico: Secretaría de Relaciones Internacionales.

Greene, James, and Brent Scowcroft, eds. 1984. *Intereses occidentales y políticas de Estados Unidos en el Caribe.* Buenos Aires: Grupo Editor Latinoamericano.

Heine, Jorge, ed. 1990. *Revolución e intervención en el Caribe: Las lecciones de Grenada.* Buenos Aires: Grupo Editor Latinoamericano.

Heine, Jorge, and Leslie Manigat, eds. 1988. *The Caribbean and World Politics.* New York: Holmes and Meier.

Ince, Basil. 1980. "Decision Making and Foreign Policy: Trinidad and Tobago's Decision to Enter the OAS." In *Issues in Caribbean International Relations,* eds. Basil Ince et al. Lanham: University Press of America.

Knight, Franklin, and Colin Palmer. 1989. *The Modern Caribbean.* Chapel Hill: University of North Carolina Press.

Lewis, David. 1991. "El sector informal y los nuevos actores sociales en el Caribe." In *El Caribe hacia el año 2000,* eds. Andrés Serbin and Anthony Bryan. Caracas: INVESP/Nueva Sociedad.

Lewis, David. 1993. "Las posibilidades de cooperación entre Centroamérica y el Caribe." Paper presented at the 4th Conference of the Association of Caribbean Economists, Curaçao, June 22-25.

Maingot, Anthony. 1983. "Cuba and the Commonwealth Caribbean: Playing the Cuban Card." In *The New Cuban Presence in the Caribbean,* ed. Barry Levine. Boulder, Colo.: Westview.

Maingot, Anthony. 1984. "Las percepciones como realidades: EE.UU., Venezuela y Cuba en el Caribe." In *Entre la autonomía y la subordinación. Política exterior de los países latinoamericanos,* eds. Heraldo Muñoz and Joseph Tulchin. Buenos Aires: Grupo Editor Latinoamericano.

Maingot, Anthony. 1992. "Cuba and CARICOM. Prospects and Risks." *CARICOM Perspective* 54- 55 (January-June): 9-12.

Maira, Luis. 1983. "Caribbean State Systems and Middle-Status Powers: The Cases of Mexico, Venezuela and Cuba." In *The Newer Caribbean. Decolonization, Democracy and Development,* eds. Henry Paget and Carl Stone. Philadelphia: Institute for the Study of Human Issues.

Manigat, Leslie. 1983. "Geopolítica de las relaciones entre Venezuela y el Caribe: problemática general y problemas." In *Geopolítica de las relaciones de Venezuela con el Caribe,* ed. Andrés Serbin. Caracas: Fondo Editorial Acta Científica.

Paget, Henry, and Carl Stone, eds. 1983. *The Newer Caribbean. Decolonization, Democracy and Development.* Philadelphia: Institute for the Study of Human Issues.

Rodríguez Beruff, Jorge, J. Peter Figueroa, and J. Edward Greene, eds. 1991. *Conflict, Peace and Development in the Caribbean.* London: Macmillan.

Sankatsing, Glenn. 1990. "Cultura y educación en las percepciones recíprocas." In *Vecinos indiferentes? El Caribe de habla inglesa y América Latina,* eds. Andrés Serbin and Anthony Bryan. Caracas: INVESP/Nueva Sociedad.

Serbin, Andrés, ed. 1983. *Geopolítica de las relaciones de Venezuela con el Caribe.* Caracas: Fondo Editorial Acta Científica.

Serbin, Andrés. 1985. "Procesos etnoculturales y percepciones mutuas en el desarrollo de las relaciones entre el Caribe de habla inglesa y América Latina," *Bulletin of Latin American and Caribbean Studies* (Amsterdam), 38(June).

Serbin, Andrés. 1987. "Venezuela ante el Caribe de habla inglesa: categorizaciones y contrastes cognitivos." In *Venezuela y las relaciones internacionales en la Cuenca del Caribe*, ed. Andrés Serbin. Caracas: ILDIS/AVECA.

Serbin, Andrés. 1989a. *El Caribe: Zona de paz?* Caracas: Comisión Sudamericana de Paz/Nueva Sociedad.

Serbin, Andrés. 1989b. "Race and Politics: Relations Between the English-Speaking Caribbean and Latin America." *Caribbean Affairs* (Port of Spain) 2 (4): 146-169.

Serbin, Andrés. 1990. *Caribbean Geopolitics: Toward Security Through Peace?* Boulder, Colo.: Lynne Rienner.

Serbin, Andrés. 1991a. "El Caribe: Mitos, realidades y desafíos para el año 2000." In *El Caribe hacia el año 2000*, eds. Andrés Serbin and Anthony Bryan. Caracas: INVESP/Nueva Sociedad.

Serbin, Andrés. 1991b. "The CARICOM States and the Group of Three: A New Partnership Between Latin America and the Non-Hispanic Caribbean?" *Journal of Interamerican Studies and World Affairs* 33 (2): 53-80.

Serbin, Andrés. 1992a. "Menage a trois ou partouze? The United States, the Caribbean and Latin America in the 90's." *Caribbean Affairs* 5 (2): 70-80.

Serbin, Andrés, ed. 1992b. *Medio ambiente, seguridad y cooperación regional en el Caribe*. Caracas: INVESP/Nueva Sociedad.

Serbin, Andrés. 1993a. *Etnocentrismo y geopolítica. Las relaciones entre el Caribe de habla inglesa y América Latina*. Caracas: Academia Nacional de la Historia.

Serbin, Andrés. 1993b. "The Group of Three: Political Cooperation, Trade Liberalization and Regionalism in the Caribbean Basin." Paper presented to the 34th Meeting of the International Studies Association, Acapulco, March 23-27.

Serbin, Andrés. 1994a. "Transnational Relations and Regionalism in the Caribbean." *The Annals of the American Academy of Political and Social Science* 533 (May): 139-150.

Serbin, Andrés. 1994b. "Integración y relaciones transnacionales: el entramado social del proceso de regionalización en la Cuenca del Caribe." *Perfiles Latinoamericanos* (Mexico) 3(4), 7-36.

Serbin, Andrés. 1994c. "Reconfirmaciones geoeconómicas y transiciones políticas en el Caribe de los noventa." In *El Caribe y Cuba en la postguerra fría*, eds. Andrés Serbin and Joseph Tulchin. Caracas: INVESP/Nueva Sociedad.

Serbin, Andrés, and Anthony Bryan, eds. 1990. *Vecinos indiferentes? El Caribe de habla inglesa y América Latina*. Caracas: INVESP/Nueva Sociedad.

Serbin, Andrés, and Anthony Bryan, eds. 1991. *El Caribe hacia el año 2000*. Caracas: INVESP/Nueva Sociedad.

Serbin, Andrés, and Joseph Tulchin, eds. 1994. *El Caribe y Cuba en la postguerra fría*. Caracas: INVESP/Nueva Sociedad.

Weintraub, Sidney. 1991. "The New United States Economic Initiative Toward Latin America." *Journal of Interamerican Studies and World Affairs* 33(1): 1-18.

West Indian Commission (WIC). 1992. *Time for Action*. Barbados: WIC.

Chapter Two

Culture and Education in Caribbean-Latin American Relations: A Critique

Glenn Sankatsing

The transmission of culture by way of education, both formal and informal, has been of central importance in the evolution of mutual perceptions between the English-speaking Caribbean and Latin America. Cultural and educational considerations must be taken into account in any attempt to modify or transform these perceptions. The objective of this study is to examine the most relevant factors for a strategy designed to improve mutual perceptions in order to promote closer relations between the two regions.

In one sense, we are venturing into relatively unexplored territory. When we approach the cultural dimension of relations between the English-speaking Caribbean and Latin America, we cannot count on an accepted theoretical framework for our discussion. Indeed, there is a clear tendency among scholars to interpret differences as divergences and similarities as the basis for coincidences. While it is true that an investigation of the many differences between the two subregions will contribute to our understanding of certain patterns in their relations, such an isolated investigation cannot be expected to characterize mutual perceptions. Divergences identified in terms of perceptions cannot be considered mere expressions of these differences. The differences are relevant to the extent that they are expressed in, or affect, the dynamics of the interrelationship between the two groups. As a consequence, our attention will be concentrated not so much on the observable differences (however marked) but, rather, on the ways these divergent elements are related to and influence interregional relations.

In this context, a study of the role of culture is obviously of paramount importance, partly because of its general cohesive function in social life but even more so because it defines structures and attitudes whose influence spans successive generations. The profound and long-lasting impact of cultural influences is inherent in their socialization function, molding new generations from the very moment they are born.

When we discuss culture, we are, of course, referring to a wide range of factors. For the moment, we propose to distinguish between those we regard as relatively permanent (historical or ethnocultural), which are largely responsible for current divergences between the regions, and those factors more susceptible to modification and, thus, of particular importance for any attempt to promote closer relations. Since our purpose is to contribute to closer relations, we will concentrate our attention on factors that can be modified.

With this objective in mind, this paper is organized in the following way: First, the historical background and more general cultural heritage of the two regions are considered briefly; second, the origins and characteristics of the formal educational systems are analyzed in greater detail; third, nonformal education in the socialization process is discussed, particularly the influence of the Church and the mass media; and finally, the importance of intellectuals (especially in the social sciences) and of international institutional affiliations in the molding of current perceptions are considered.

The Historical Background

Current differences between the English-speaking Caribbean and Latin America are rooted in the different effects of the English and Spanish colonial systems. Long-standing linguistic barriers, cultural idiosyncracies, and a general climate of distrust and hostility reflect the historic rivalry between England and Spain. The different colonization processes led to contrasting experiences in the formation of states and the evolution of respective societies. We can identify distinctive historical developments in the ethnocultural, sociopolitical, economic, geopolitical, and ideological fields. These have led to contrasting rhythms in the decolonization process, differences in the post-independence political systems, and dissimilar ways of relating to the metropolitan powers, both the European dating from the colonial period and the North American, which has dominated the more recent period that Henry Paget describes as marked by a process of new "peripheralization" (Paget 1985).

Transmission of Culture

During the modern period, the formal educational system has been responsible primarily for the transmission of the dominant cultural values. In a less formal way, at least from the point of view of the state, the Church and the mass media also play an important role. The Church's influence is less than in the colonial period when it was greater than that of the formal educational system. The influence of the mass media has increased to such an extent that many consider its impact comparable to that of formal education. These institutions will be examined on a comparative basis in order to ascertain their importance in the formation of perceptions between the two regions.

In societies molded by the colonial system, as was the case of the English-speaking Caribbean and Latin America, the capacity of the respective cultures to reproduce themselves has been particularly marked. The colonizing powers, in their determination to impose and consolidate their own cultural values, resorted freely to coercive measures and sanctions in order to root out potential discrepancies from the indigenous cultures. As a result, we find that not even decolonization has managed to shake the firmly rooted metropolitan culture. There was a clear change in political status and, to a lesser extent, in economic relations, but cultural values were hardly affected. Apparently, this cultural continuity has been even more marked in those colonies with a multiethnic population. In this sense, the persistence of Anglo-Saxon culture in the English-speaking Caribbean is striking. In the case of Latin America, the weight of the Spanish heritage is still evident and has been revived even during this century with a renewed emphasis on concepts such as "the Spanish world" and "hispanidad." Generally speaking, the hegemony of the colonial cultural heritage has not been questioned seriously despite different nostalgic attempts to seek more authentic roots, as in the cases of Black Power and Rastafarianism in the Caribbean and the different indigenous movements in Latin America.

This notable weight of the dominant colonial culture clearly accounts to a great extent for the sharp contemporary contrasts between the former English and Spanish colonies, not simply based on language. There are differences in cognitive styles; in short, there are differing cultural traditions defined by Edmund and Christine Glenn as "forms of thought or ways of organizing information which become habitual and which can be used in a variety of situations and with many different kinds of information" (Glenn and Glenn 1985, 12).

In both subregions, the narrow ethnocentrism imposed by the colonizing countries prevailed despite the many characteristics and interests that the regions had in common in terms of geography, economy, social reality, and strategic interests. Given their successful implantation, the Anglo-Saxon and Hispanic cultures and traditions constituted a factor that accentuated the discrepancies. Both the indigenous culture and the cultures that were introduced subsequently, along with populations from other parts of the colonized world, were relegated to a second plane. In the English-speaking Caribbean, the impact of colonial culture was particularly marked because during the first one hundred years of the English presence indigenous culture was repressed to such an extent that it disappeared without a trace. In the islands, the indigenous population simply was exterminated, while in the Guyana territories, it was forced to flee inland from the coastal settlements (Sankatsing 1989, 18-19). In Latin America, a certain synthesis was produced between the dominant Spanish culture and elements of indigenous culture, reflected in a miscegenation process and the emergence of a "criollo" culture. In the English-speaking Caribbean, however, societies were formed by incorporating an African or Afro-Indian population within the Anglo-Saxon system of domination through importation of African slaves and later immigrations from India (Serbin 1987). This complex interplay of factors widened the gap between the two subregions. The result has been contrasting ethnocultural characteristics that have influenced mutual relations: in the Caribbean, Afro-American and Indo-Caribbean elements; and in Latin America, miscegenation and persisting Amerindian influences.

Educational Developments

As is generally recognized, education plays a central role in socialization precisely because it is "the process through which new generations take possession of the cultural heritage of their community" (Larroyo 1981, 45). The educational system is the institution that exercises greatest influence in maintaining and reproducing a cultural heritage as defined by the dominant culture. But, apart from this general function, Germán Rama argues that in the case of emerging societies, it is of particular importance "for the process of nation-building, for the relations between strata and social classes, for the conformation of rational thought structures, for the reproduction of ideology and, above all, for the creation of conditions favorable to social participation" (Rama 1987, 27).

In analyzing the role of education in the region, two processes of particular importance can be distinguished for their influence upon relations between the English-speaking Caribbean and Latin America: first, the prolonged tradition of an exclusive and elitist education; and second, the recent and rapid conversion to universal education as part of a more general process of social emancipation.

Fundamental colonial interests determined a clearly elitist educational system, organized for the benefit of white children — excluding blacks, mulattoes, Amerindians, mestizos, and Indians. Until the early twentieth century, despite some limited advances in the instruction of certain strata of the colonized population, the educational system in Latin America and the Caribbean never lost its elitist character (Rama 1987). This characteristic is reflected by the fact that "in Latin America the university was created before the rest of the educational system and during a prolonged period it was the only institution which imparted post-secondary teaching" (Franco Arbaláez and Tunnerman Blénheim 1978, 167). This is in evident contrast with the development of the educational system in Europe, where educating the masses through the primary levels preceded the systematic establishment of secondary and university education by the state (Filgueira 1980, 56).

As was to be expected in settlement colonies, universities founded as early as the sixteenth century were typically colonial institutions that did not envisage inclusion of the colonized peoples. The latter were controlled basically by naked repression. Despite the restricted elitist nature of the Latin American universities, we find that when Harvard University was founded in North America in 1636, Latin America contained thirteen universities (Franco and Tunnerman 1978, 168).

In the English-speaking Caribbean, which was not made up of settlement colonies but rather of what Lloyd Best defines as "hinterlands of exploitation," the development of higher education took more time (Best 1968). An initial attempt was the opening of Codrington College in Barbados in 1830,[1] but it was not until 1948 that the University College of the West Indies was founded in Jamaica, laying the basis for the subsequent development of a university system throughout the English-speaking Caribbean.

In both subregions, the universities were not only elitist; they were also faithful copies of established institutions in their respective colonial metropolises. In the case of the English-speaking Caribbean, the University College of the West Indies was an overseas College of London University. On the other hand, Darcy Ribeiro points out, "The Latin American university was a replica of the Hispanic model of higher education: aristocratic, scholastic, and clerical" (Ribeiro 1973, 77). In fact, the universities founded in Latin America were modeled on the two most renowned Spanish universities, Salamanca and Alcalá de Henares (Franco and Tunnerman 1978, 168).

This characteristic of the Latin American universities is reflected in the role they played in the face of social change during the colonial period. For instance, in the seventeenth century, when the "hacienda" was replacing the "encomienda" and a "criollo" consciousness of being "American" began to emerge (Steger 1974, 208-209), no parallel change can be detected in the universities. In fact, the inertia of these educational institutions meant that they "lost their pivotal role in social developments" (Steger 1974, 211-218).

The exclusive, elitist character of the colonial educational system naturally reproduced and even accentuated the gulf between the colonizers and the rest of the population precisely because it was designed exclusively to transmit the dominant colonial culture. The exclusion of the mass of the population is a simple expression of one of the central characteristics of the colonial system, summed up by Germán Rama in terms of "the construction of the state prior to the formation of the nation." In these circumstances, it was perfectly natural to find "excluded from power those who had never really been convoked to exercise it" (Rama 1987, 49).

During the course of several centuries, rudimentary higher education in the Caribbean was restricted to the free white community, as was to be expected in a slave society based on racial discrimination (Braithwaite 1965,

76 and 1958, 52). As Errol Miller has commented, "The plantation society was autocratic. There was no room for dissidence, dialogue, or even enlightened doubt. Production in the plantation required a large, non-qualified and cheap labor force...." As a result, for this labor force "education was regarded as subversive" (Miller 1988, 2). In the case of Latin America, the legacy of their elitist educational system was that as late as 1950 half of the adult population was still illiterate (Rama 1987, 2).

From the beginning of the twentieth century, economic and social developments in both regions favored a greater amplitude in the educational system as a result of economic expansion and accelerated urbanization. Nevertheless, the universality of educational systems has occurred much more recently. In both the English-speaking Caribbean and Latin America, the dramatic expansion of the system took place after the Second World War. Mass education was also accompanied by a qualitative change reflected in the introduction of new disciplines and a clearer differentiation between levels within the system. It was precisely in this epoch when the University of the West Indies (1962) and the University of Guyana (1963) were founded.[2]

In the case of higher education in Latin America, the 1918 Córdoba reform spearheaded a renovation of the system. The Córdoba Manifesto led, among other things, to the introduction of university autonomy and the election of university authorities by representative assemblies (Ribeiro 1971, 152-153). This reform, in turn, facilitated the later process of liberalization in two ways: New social sectors were given access to higher education, and there was a new acceptance of pluralism as intrinsic to the nature of the institution.

After the Second World War, there was another significant advance. The "massive institutionalization of the social sciences in the majority of the Latin American countries" (Sonntag 1988, 70) reflected a greater involvement of the universities in social questions. These tendencies were reinforced in the 1960s and 1970s to such an extent that Carlos Filguiera could comment that during these decades "education has provided the most important channel for social mobility in the region" (Filgueira 1980, 50). This resulted from the educational system's expansion registering "rates that were exceptionally elevated, compared with any other region of the world, or with any historical precedent. In a few decades, the region underwent a transformation which in many developed countries had taken more than a hundred years" (Filgueira 1980, 47).

This rapid conversion to mass education after a prolonged period of elitist education, common to the two regions, undoubtedly affected the divergences and mutual perceptions. While, as we have seen, the previous tradition of elitist education had contributed to negative mutual perceptions between the two regions by imposing patterns that responded to the prejudices, differences, and controversies between the two rival metropolises, the later conversion of the educational systems, to the extent that it tended to weaken the reproduction and transmission of colonial culture and values, at least opened up a greater space for other cultural expressions previously repressed by the dominant culture. Despite the rapid opening of educational opportunities, the impact of education on mutual perceptions naturally has been a more gradual process. Universal education has, nevertheless, been a positive factor to the extent that it has stimulated greater awareness of the social and economic problems common to the two regions, thus establishing new points of convergence. In this sense, the relatively new universal nature of the educational systems has created a context potentially more favorable for closer relations between the regions.

Beyond the general coincidence in the rhythm of changes from an elitist to a mass educational system, we need to register marked differences between the regions in terms of the degree of autonomous initiatives vis-à-vis the respective colonial traditions or in relation to what we can call the "indigenization" of their educational systems. In the case of Latin America, we find that parallel to the independence struggle in the early nineteenth century, "the first attempts to reform the educational system, independently of the Hispanic tradition, were undertaken" (Steger 1974, 94). By way of contrast, in the case of the English-speaking Caribbean, the educational system continued to be based on a simple copy of the British organizational structure and curriculum until quite recently. But even now it has not altogether freed itself of these foreign influences. Of course, the reduced size of the Caribbean micro-states favors the persistence of inherited colonial influences and limits the prospects of developing systems genuinely inspired in local values. However, an important advance is that "the approbation of students graduating from secondary schools is based on examinations designed and controlled by the Caribbean Examination Board, which will gradually assume responsibility for all examinations at the secondary level" (Carrington 1987, 134).

This contrast between the two regions is largely a result of the different nature of their respective colonial systems and, above all, of the time lag between the expansive cycles of the two empires. The relative weakness of Spain from the seventeenth century on, which reduced it to the category of "a feudal state of southern Europe" (Stone 1983, 14), increasingly limited its capacity to maintain a tight political and cultural control over Latin America, a situation clearly reflected in the loss of its Empire at the outset of the nineteenth century. Latin America achieved its independence precisely when the British Empire was consolidating its position as the major world power. For this reason, the possibility of independence in the English-speaking Caribbean was not envisaged in the nineteenth century, and in the twentieth century, its advocates eschewed any radical confrontation with the colonial power. When the British recognized the convenience of conceding political independence on the basis of peaceful negotiations that culminated in the 1960s, they left no space for the emergence of a militant anti-colonial movement (Sankatsing 1989, 24).

These contrasting experiences, with their profound cultural roots, have marked the respective educational systems and social thought of the two regions and thus have been of fundamental importance in the molding of perceptions.

Non-formal Education

B eyond the formal educational structures, the two most important institutions for the molding of attitudes and opinions are the Church and the mass media.

As far as the influence of the Church is concerned, formal and informal education are difficult to distinguish because ecclesiastical education is conceived of as an integral part of religious function. The influence of the Church in educational development in the hemisphere has not been uniform. In both subregions, the Church has participated in the institutionalization of teaching from the outset until the present. In the case of Latin America, colonial education was confessional and for a long time was a virtual Church monopoly. Larroyo identifies "a characteristic type of confessional education in which everything is understood in terms of a religious ideal." Furthermore, he argues, "this clearly ecclesiastical stage persists until well into the Independence period" (Larroyo 1981, 24). Despite the controversial positions occasionally assumed by the Church, religion and education have been powerful instruments in the imposition of Spanish culture upon the indigenous populations of Latin America (Vázquez 1975).

In the case of the English-speaking Caribbean, the Church was also involved in education, although compared with Latin America the process developed later, and the presence of the Church was less marked. In any event, the fundamental difference was that in the English-speaking Caribbean, it was the Anglican Church that exercised its influence and not the Catholic Church, except in the case of Trinidad and Tobago. Furthermore, in two countries of the English-speaking Caribbean, there is also a significant presence of Hinduism and Islam. People of Indian descent are the largest ethnic group in Guyana, and they account for more than one-third of the population in Trinidad and Tobago.

As a result of the significant impact of religion in the social, cultural, intellectual, and ideological life of the community, religious diversity contributed to a differentiation of the English-speaking Caribbean from Latin America. It has contributed to the respective perceptions of the two subregions.

In the field of non-formal education, the mass media also play an important role, especially in relation to the international flow of information. In general, the fact that control of the international mass media is in the hands of foreigners, as a result of the overall technological dependency of the region, means that the predominant cultural influence is transnational, dominated by the United States and Europe. As a result, the mass media cannot be expected to serve as a channel for furthering communication and understanding between the two regions. Nevertheless, there is an increasing tendency toward uniformity between the two regions as a result of the "integrating capacity of the modern system of mass communications" (Unión de Universidades 1972, 214-215). But this does not necessarily mean a greater convergence between the two subregions because the selection of news to be distributed is adapted to their respective idiosyncracies. This seriously limits the possibilities of modifying existing perceptions by way of the mass media, because direct communication is very limited and the news is generally filtered by the international news networks. For this reason, greater uniformity and mutual understanding, as a result of the influence of the mass media, represent little more than a common experience of the "Americanization" of their respective societies.

Furthermore, within the national context, the prevalent mercantilist logic points in the same direction; liberty of expression is generally understood as freedom for business interests, and it proves difficult to establish an alternative that responds to a public interest (Oficina de Estudios Socioeconómicos 1970-1975). In such circumstances, these societies continue to be vulnerable, particularly to external influences and to a cultural colonialism imposed by the developed countries.

Social Thought and the Role of Intellectuals

The evolution of social thought in Latin America and the Caribbean has been profoundly marked by European influences since the beginning of the colonial era, because of constant contacts with the philosophical currents that prospered on the European continent in successive epochs. In the fields of education and science, this influence meant an accentuated Euro-centrism in the region which, in turn, constituted an essential dimension of the prevailing cultural colonialism.

In her analysis of ideas in Latin America, Isabel Monal observes, "The philosophical tendencies which took root in our continent after the pre-Columbian period to a large extent reflected the influence of different European currents" (Monal 1985, 13). As an explanation of the weakness of the indigenous tradition, she suggests that "evangelization implied a struggle against the entire spiritual heritage of the underdeveloped peoples" (Monal 1985, 43). In the English-speaking Caribbean, we have seen how the indigenous culture was repressed to such an extent that its influence was virtually eliminated. This, together with the absence of a local scientific or intellectual tradition, meant that the basis was lacking for an indigenous culture capable of providing a counterweight to the social thought and social sciences imported from the metropolis.[3]

Although social thought in the Caribbean was permanently nourished from European sources, it cannot be treated as a simple transplant, thoroughly alien to the local society. Any such posture rests on an artificial dichotomy between the "external" and the "internal" and fails to take into account the dialectical process by which external influences are adapted to, and become an integral part of, the local dynamic (Sankatsing 1989, 15). In the case of Latin America, this goes without saying because, as Monal has pointed out, one can observe a close relationship between the advances in social thought and the development of the society itself, a relationship clearly influenced by the "fundamental events in political and economic affairs" (Monal 1985, 22).

But even in the English-speaking Caribbean, which felt the weight of the colonial cultural presence with particular force, any interpretation that limits the analysis to foreign influences overlooks "a tradition of continuous intellectual debate on political issues stretching back to the eighteenth century and even beyond" (Benn 1987, 162). Indeed, there is already a substantial literature that demonstrates the original contributions of the Caribbean to the development of social thought.[4]

As we have noted in so many other areas, the contributions of Latin America and the English-speaking Caribbean to social thought developed for many years along parallel lines that precluded mutual contacts and influences. It is only during recent decades that we can discern common themes and the beginnings of reciprocal influences. In the social sciences, after the Second World War the theoretical positions assumed by the Economic Commission for Latin America (ECLA) began to have an impact on thought in the English-speaking Caribbean. Anthony Bryan has underlined the importance for intellectual thought in the Caribbean of Latin American authors such as Celso Furtado and Raúl Prebisch, particularly in the case of analyses of the role of transnational companies (Bryan 1983, 4). However, Norman Girvan, one of the leaders of the "New World Group" that brought together a new generation of critical social scientists in the English-speaking Caribbean and dominated thought on economics and development in the 1960s and 1970s, has argued that the reflections on underdevelopment in Latin America and the English-speaking Caribbean "emerged virtually independently of one another" (Girvan 1973, 1). Girvan's interpretation has been criticized severely by various authors, including George Cumper, Hilbourne Watson, and Ivar Oxaal.[5]

Whatever the precise degree of contact and mutual influence in this particular case, what appears undeniable, as has been suggested by Bryan, is that intellectuals are capable of assuming an important role in the search for closer relations between the two regions. In fact, Bryan comments, "It is the intellectuals in the Caribbean and Latin America who are the main proponents of regional integration, while businessmen and politicians continue to show studied ambivalence" (Bryan 1983, 12-13).

However, Caribbean intellectuals have contributed to a widening of the breach between the two regions. The most notable is the late Trinidadian historian Eric Williams, who enjoyed an undeniable prestige in the region both as an intellectual and as a prominent politician who served as his country's head of government for a quarter of a century.[6] Williams adopted a definition of the Caribbean that explicitly excluded the non-insular Latin American countries with Caribbean coasts. This reaction was a consequence first of the small size of the English-speaking Caribbean countries and their increasing distrust of the Latin American middle powers that had begun to make their presence felt in the Caribbean. Second, Williams' view reflected the geopolitical changes implicit in the process of decolonization, with a reduction of the traditional colonial influence in the region and, as a corollary, greater space for the activities of nontraditional regional actors. These factors, the reduced size of the Caribbean countries and the geopolitical changes, were also felt in the fields of education and culture, particularly when Latin American cultural centers began to proliferate in the region (for example, the Venezuelan "Andrés Bello" Cultural Centers).

In sum, the influence of the respective colonial cultural heritages upon social thought in Latin America and the English-speaking Caribbean constituted a formidable obstacle to communication and understanding between the two regions and contributed decisively to the divergent paths they took toward mutual isolation. Only after the Second World War were there clear signs of an exchange of information and an opening up of channels of communication, as in the social sciences.

International Educational Orientations

There are three types of international activities that we consider relevant for our discussion of mutual perceptions between the two regions: 1) the external orientation of the respective educational systems and the cultural impact of migratory flows; 2) participation in international organizations as a source of possible coincidences or divergences; and 3) the implications of foreign control of the international mass media.

Historically, relations between the two regions in the fields of higher education and the social sciences have been limited by the fact that both regions' links traditionally have been with the industrialized countries. Latin American universities have established links most frequently with the United States and Canada (68 percent) and secondly with Western Europe (54 percent), while contacts between institutions within the region have been much less frequent (Soria et al. 1985, 112). The persistence of this pattern suggests the need to intensify intraregional scientific relations. It is evident, however, that prospects for greater integration or cooperation in the field of education, particularly between universities, form part of the more general problem of promoting regional integration. This became evident in the University of the West Indies, which suffered a series of problems as a result of the failure of the West Indian Federation (Sankatsing 1989, 47-48).

During the colonial epoch and until quite recently, there was a tradition among the upper classes of the English-speaking Caribbean "of sending their children abroad for higher and, in some cases, secondary education" (Braithwaite 1965, 77). One effect of this tradition "was to tie the educational system of these colonies, at all levels, to a foreign rather than an indigenous culture" (Braithwaite 1965, 77).

In the English-speaking Caribbean, as in Latin America, the presence of migrant communities in the metropolitan countries exercises an important influence on their external orientation. Massive emigration from the English-speaking Caribbean to England, Canada, and the United States and the existence in those countries of Caribbean communities promoted greater intercommunication and a certain cultural integration with these nations. The situation of Latin American migrants is not strictly comparable because the various communities that have settled in the metropolitan countries tend to maintain a greater degree of autonomy and internal cohesion and thus serve less as a bridge between the host country's culture and their own. It is worth considering the extent to which relations between Caribbean and Latin American communities within the metropolitan countries could become closer were there greater opportunities for interaction. Or, on the contrary, could such contacts provoke tensions produced by a competition for opportunities within the new context?

Migrations between the two regions have been important in different eras, and cultural differences "have not impeded large popular migrations from some Caribbean Commonwealth countries like Jamaica to continental countries such as Costa Rica and Panama which needed surplus manpower" (Lewis 1984, 183). But these migratory flows, motivated strictly by economic considerations, have not had important repercussions in the cultural sphere.

In international cultural relations, membership in organizations that reflect common interests opens up the prospect of improving mutual perceptions. Of course, potentially negative effects are to be expected in cases where the interests of two regions diverge or even conflict.

The participation of the English-speaking Caribbean countries in the Organization of American States, beginning with Trinidad and Tobago and Barbados in 1967 and followed by Jamaica in 1969 and Grenada in 1975, opened the path to an incorporation of this region into joint activities in the educational field, as in the case of the Regional Program for Educational Development, a multinational, inter-American cooperation and mutual aid force (Allard 1978, 34). Trinidad and Tobago was the first English-speaking Caribbean beneficiary in 1970 (Alleyne 1978, 34). The founding of the Caribbean Universities and Research Institutes Association (UNICA) in November 1968 laid the basis for increasing exchanges within the Caribbean, helping to overcome the language barriers. The association managed to maintain an activity that averaged six events a year, including forums, work groups, meetings of specialists, seminars and conferences, and the regular publication of the *Caribbean Educational Bulletin.*[7]

This increased contact in the cultural sphere was related to other developments, such as the growth in trade between Latin America and the English-speaking Caribbean and a renewed interest in Caribbean studies on the part of Latin American specialists (Mathews 1979). The joint activities of Caribbean and Latin American countries within the Latin American Economic System (SELA) and the observer status within CARICOM granted to Venezuela, the Dominican Republic, and Colombia provide greater opportunities for closer relations and cooperation. Conversely, the participation of the English-speaking countries in the Commonwealth of Nations, as well as the exclusion of the Latin American states from the ACP Group (Africa, Caribbean, Pacific) and initially from the Lomé Conventions, introduced a competitive element that accentuated the differences between the two regions and introduced elements that inhibited closer interregional relations.[8]

Conclusions

The nature of mutual perceptions between Latin America and the English-speaking Caribbean is the result of a multitude of factors that can be divided into two broad categories. First, there are those relatively invariable elements of an historical or ethnocultural nature that form the sociohistorical context within which current perceptions have been molded. Second, there are those variables that are more susceptible to change over time and thus to modifications that could improve reciprocal images. In this second group, elements related to formal and informal education have been examined.

In our analysis of educational developments in the two regions, we have highlighted two processes that have affected mutual perceptions in contrasting ways: elitist education and its subsequent conversion to mass education. While the elitist education tended to accentuate discrepancies between the two regions, because it served to reproduce the dominant culture of each of the respective colonial countries, educating all of the people has tended to weaken the capacity of colonial cultures to impose themselves, opening up a space for more authentic cultural expressions and a greater awareness of the socioeconomic problems that the regions have in common.

In order to promote a closer relationship between the two regions, there is an evident role in the educational field for common policies and actions that undoubtedly would favor more positive mutual perceptions. On the basis of this analysis, we can suggest some potential fields of action.

First, the historical orientation of the educational systems and their curricula toward the metropolises needs to be reoriented in order to increase mutual knowledge between the two regions in the fields of culture, history, and geography. At the same time, the educational systems could contribute to overcoming the language barrier by promoting the study of second languages from the region.

Second, the mass media's contribution to the formation of images, attitudes, and prejudices is evidently of central importance. The fact that these media are largely in foreign hands has had negative effects on the information flow between the two regions. In consequence, any policy designed to promote closer relations must question the status quo in relation to ownership and control of the industry. There must be initiatives designed to favor greater local control in this field.

Third, as far as international relations are concerned, there is still room for greater collaboration in the educational field, especially in higher education. Beyond the positive initiative that led to the foundation of UNICA, there remains a tremendous potential for cooperative programs between universities, exchanges of professors and students, joint research, and other activities in common.

Fourth, in order to adapt scientific research to regional needs, new ways of channeling available aid and collaboration are an urgent priority. Consequently, the intellectual elites of the two regions, who form a cultural vanguard, ought to assume a more dynamic role in academic, cultural, and political activities in order to contribute to the solution of common socioeconomic problems and respond to the pressures to which both regions are now subject due to the accelerating rhythm of global changes.

We are well aware that existing perceptions are not easily modified and that they are often slow to respond to changing circumstances. However, there do exist real possibilities for action in the cultural field geared to promoting mutual perceptions more favorable than those inherited from the past. It is for this reason that cultural activity requires a clear regional perspective, both in Latin America and the English-speaking Caribbean, and needs to be designed consciously in order to promote mutual understanding. The full fruits of such a process will mature only in the long run.

Notes

1. See Braithwaite 1958 and Lane 1989.

2. See Williams and Harvey 1985; and Fletcher, France, and Sukdoe 1987.

3. This point is analyzed at greater length in another publication of the author. See Sankatsing 1989, 19.

4. We refer to the following works: Goveia 1984 (original in 1956);La Guerre 1982; Lewis 1983; Benn 1987.

5. Cumper declares emphatically that Girvan exaggerates the extent of his independence of these influences: see Cumper 1974; Hilbourne Watson also criticizes him on the grounds that he "drew eclectically from the nationalist and neo-Marxist traditions in Latin America": see Watson 1986, 225. For his part, Oxaal claims that "the West Indian radical academic economists occupy an elite position not totally dissimilar from the social science technicians in Latin America (...)" because "their politics may appear revolutionary in their external aspects, but are reformist with respect to internal social changes"; see Oxaal 1975.

6. Eric Williams was one of the pioneers in social science in the Caribbean who published several very influential scholarly works even while he was Prime Minister of Trinidad and Tobago.

7. The *Caribbean Educational Bulletin* has provided extensive information on UNICA. For a general evaluation, see vol. XX, No. 3, September 1983.

8. Manigat 1988, 354. Subsequently, the Lomé IV Convention was extended to include the Dominican Republic, Haiti, and Suriname.

References

Allard, Raúl. 1978. "La primera década del PREDE: Perspectivas futuras," *La Educación: Revista Interamericana de Desarrollo Educativo* XXII (78-80).

Alleyne, Michael. 1978. "The PREDE in the English-speaking Caribbean," *La Educación: Revista Interamericana de Desarrollo Educativo* XXII (78-80).

Benn, Denis. 1987. *Ideology and Political Development: The Growth and Development of Political Ideas in the Caribbean, 1774-1983.* Kingston: Institute of Social and Economic Studies.

Best, Lloyd. 1968. "Outlines of a Model of Pure Plantation Economy," *Social and Economic Studies* 17 (3).

Braithwaite, Lloyd. 1958. "The Development of Higher Education in the British West Indies," *Social and Economic Studies* 7 (1).

Braithwaite, Lloyd. 1965. "The Role of the University in the Developing Society of the West Indies," *Social and Economic Studies* 14 (1).

Brown, Aggrey, ed. 1984. *La irrupción del Caribe.* Caracas: Editorial Nueva Sociedad.

Bryan, Anthony. 1983. "The CARICOM and Latin American Integration Experiences: Observations on Theoretical Origins and Comparative Performance," *CARICOM Bulletin* 4.

Caribbean Educational Bulletin (The). 1983. XX (3), September.

Carrington, Lawrence C. 1980. "La educación en el Caribe de habla inglesa." In *Educación y sociedad en América Latina y el Caribe,* ed. Germán W. Rama. Santiago de Chile: UNICEF.

Cumper, George. 1974. "Dependence, Development, and the Sociology of Economic Thought," *Social and Economic Studies* 3 (3).

Filgueira, Carlos. 1980. "Expansión educacional y estratificación social en América Latina (1960-1979)." In *Educación y sociedad en América Latina y el Caribe,* ed. Germán W. Rama. Santiago de Chile: UNICEF.

Fletcher, Gem, Lynette France, and Iris D. Sukdoe. 1987. *Higher Education in Guyana.* Caracas: CRESALC-UNESCO.

Franco Arbaláez, Augusto, and Tunnerman Blénheim, Carlos. 1978. *La educación superior en la perspectiva mundial y latinoamericana.* Cali: Fundación para la Educación Superior.

Girvan, Norman. 1973. "The Development of Dependency Economics in the Caribbean and Latin America: Review and Comparison," *Social and Economic Studies* 22 (1).

Glenn, Edmund S., and Christine Glenn. 1985 (English original 1981). *El hombre y la humanidad: Conflicto y communicación entre culturas.* Buenos Aires: Editorial Piadós.

Goveia, Elsa. 1984 (original 1956). *Estudios de la historiografía de las Antillas inglesas hasta finales del siglo XIX*. Havana: Casa de las Américas.

Heine, Jorge, and Leslie Manigat, eds. 1988. *The Caribbean and World Politics: Cross Currents and Cleavages*. New York: Holmes and Meier.

La Guerre, John G. 1982. *The Social and Political Thought of the Colonial Intelligentsia*. Kingston: ISER.

Lane, Anthony. 1989. *Higher Education in Barbados*. Caracas: CRESALC-UNESCO.

Larroyo, Francisco. 1981 (original 1941). *Historia comparada de la educación en México*. Mexico: Editorial Porrúa.

Lewis, Gordon K. 1983. *Main Currents in Caribbean Thought: The Historical Evolution of Caribbean Society in its Ideological Aspects, 1492-1900*. Kingston: Heinemann Educational Books.

Lewis, Vaughan. 1984. "Los países de la mancomunidad caribeña, la descolonización y el realineamiento diplomático: Relaciones con las potencias intermedias del hemisferio." In *La irrupción del Caribe*, ed. Aggrey Brown. Caracas: Editorial Nueva Sociedad.

Manigat, Leslie. 1988. "The Caribbean Between Global Horizons and Latin American Perspectives." In *The Caribbean and World Politics: Cross Currents and Cleavages,* eds. Jorge Heine and Leslie Manigat. New York: Holmes and Meier.

Mathews, Thomas. 1979. *The Increased Interest in Caribbean Studies in the Spanish-speaking Caribbean*. Austin, Texas: SALALM Secretariat, University of Texas Library.

Miller, Errol. 1988. "The Latent Potency of Education. The Post-Emancipation Education: Legacy to the Twentieth Century," mimeo. Kingston: Faculty of Education UWI.

Monal, Isabel. 1985. "Las ideas en América Latina: Una antología del pensamiento filosófico, político y social." In *Del pensamiento precolombino al sensualismo*, vol. 1, ed. Isabel Monal. Havana: Casa de las Américas.

Oficina de Estudios Socioeconómicos. 1970-1975. *Los mensajes peligrosos: Un estudio sobre los medios masivos de comunicación social y sus efectos en la sociedad actual, especialmente en Venezuela*. Caracas: Oficina de Estudios Socioeconómicos.

Oxaal, Ivar. 1975. "The Dependency Economist as Grassroots Politician in the Caribbean." In *Beyond the Sociology of Development,* eds. Ivar Oxaal, Tony Barnett, and David Boots. London: Routledge and Kegan Paul.

Paget, Henry. 1985. *Peripheral Capitalism and Underdevelopment in Antigua*. New Brunswick, N.J.: Transaction Books.

Rama, Germán W., ed. 1980. *Educación y sociedad en América Latina y el Caribe*. Santiago de Chile: UNICEF.

Rama, Germán W. 1987. "Educación y sociedad en América Latina," *Revista Interamericana de Desarrollo Educativo* XXXI (101).

Ribeiro, Darcy. 1971. *La universidad latinoamericana*. Santiago de Chile: Editorial Universitaria.

Ribeiro, Darcy. 1973. *La universidad nueva: Un proyecto*. Buenos Aires: Editorial Ciencia Nueva.

Sankatsing, Glenn. 1989. *Caribbean Social Science: An Assessment*. Caracas: UNESCO.

Serbin, Andrés. 1987. *Etnicidad, clase y nación en la cultura política del Caribe de habla inglesa*. Caracas: Academia Nacional de Historia.

Sonntag, Heinz R. 1988. *Duda/Certeza/Crisis: La evolución de las ciencias sociales de América Latina*. Caracas: UNESCO-Editorial Nueva Sociedad.

Soria, Oscar N., et al. 1985. "Las relaciones internacionales de las universidades de América Latina y el Caribe," *Docencia Postsecondaria* 13 (2).

Steger, Hans-Albert. 1974 (original German 1967). *Las universidades en el desarrollo social de América Latina*. Mexico City: Fondo de Cultura Económica.

Stone, Carl. 1983. "Patterns of Insertion into the World Economy: Historical Profiles and Contemporary Options," *Social and Economic Studies* 32 (3).

Unión de Universidades de América Latina. 1972. *La difusión cultural y la extensión universitaria en el cambio social de América Latina*. Mexico: Unión de Universidades de América Latina.

Vázquez, Josefina Z. 1975. "El pensamiento renacentista español y los orígenes de la educación novohispana." In *Nacionalismo y educación en Mexico*, second edition, ed. Josefina Z. Vázquez. Mexico: El Colegio de Mexico.

Watson, Hilbourne A. 1986. "Economic Dependency and Geopolitics: Recurring Ideological Themes in Caribbean Intellectual Culture," *New West Indies Guide* 60 (3-4).

Williams, Gwendoline, and Claudia Harvey. 1985. *Higher Education in Trinidad and Tobago: A Focus on Organizational Development and Change*. Caracas: CRESALC-UNESCO.

Chapter Three

National Identity and Race in Latin America and the Caribbean: A Comparative Analysis

Francine Jácome

Ethnic and racial diversity in Latin America and the Caribbean (see Tables 1 and 2) are the results of dissimilar colonial experiences.[1] Before colonization, extensive parts of Latin America were occupied by indigenous populations with varying degrees of economic and cultural development, exemplified by Mexico and Peru. In other regions, such as Venezuela and Brazil and, to a lesser extent, Colombia and the Dominican Republic, the Amerindian population was scarce and lived in relatively isolated communities. In Mexico and Peru, the population was conquered and transformed into a rural labor force; in the other regions, it was generally exterminated or forced to seek refuge in the most isolated zones. As a result, in countries such as Venezuela and Brazil, the development of plantation economies required imported slave labor from Africa.

The English-speaking Caribbean was characterized by an economic organization structured around sugar production, based on the plantation system and slave labor. Initially, there was an attempt to submit the scarce indigenous population to the rigors of the plantation system, but the result was their extermination and the need to import workers from Africa.[2]

The nature of these colonization processes meant that the emerging system of social stratification was intimately linked to racial and ethnic differences. Both in Latin America and the English-speaking Caribbean, the white colonizers made up a dominant elite that exploited and controlled the black slaves and Amerindian workers. At the same time, a predominantly white intermediate sector began to emerge, made up of colonial administration employees and those who worked in the commercial and service sectors. The miscegenation process,[3] which took place to a much greater extent in Latin America than in the English-speaking Caribbean, led to the incorporation of some relatively light-skinned mestizos and mulattoes into this intermediate

Table 1.
Racial Composition of the Population in Latin America
Percentages

	Indo-american	Black	Mestizo	Mulatto	White
Brazil	2	8	—	30	60
Colombia	2.2	6	47.8	24	28
Cuba	—	12.4	—	17.3	70
Dominican Republic	—	12	—	60	28
Mexico	29	—	55	—	16
Puerto Rico	—	—	—	*25	75
Venezuela**	2-5	3-10	60-90	4-17	10-25

* = In this case, the source registers blacks and mulattoes together.
** = A rough calculation because since the 1926 census, racial characteristics have not been registered.
Source: *Geografía de América*, 1984, (Barcelona: Ediciones Océano).

Table 2.
Racial Composition of the Population in the
English-speaking Caribbean
Percentages

	Black	Mulatto	White	Indians	Others
Barbados	77	18	5	—	—
Grenada	52.7	42.2	—	—	6.3
Guyana*	31	10	0.5	52	6.5
Jamaica	77	19	1	—	3
Trinidad & Tobago	43	16	3	36	2

* = From Andrés Serbin, 1987, *Etnicidad, clase y cultura en la cultura política del Caribe de habla inglesa* (Caracas: Biblioteca de la Academia de la Historia).
Source: *Geografía de América*, 1984 (Barcelona: Ediciones Océano).

strata. However, the great majority of mestizos and mulattoes, together with the Amerindian population and the blacks, remained submerged among the dominated majority in these predominantly non-white societies.

The abolition of slavery had little impact on the status of blacks, given that legal emancipation had limited social consequences. Nevertheless, it must be noted that in the Caribbean colonized by the British, differentiation between whites and blacks was particularly marked, precisely because of the absence of an important intermediate group of mulattoes.

As a consequence of the independence struggle in Latin America and the concomitant violent rupture with the colonial power, the new political elite throughout the region was obliged to form alliances with the mestizo and mulatto groups and to seek support for their projected autonomy among the Amerindian and black population on the basis of an ideology of national integration. The need to seek support among these groups also led to the incorporation of mestizos and mulattoes into the new elite, especially in countries such as Mexico, Colombia, and Venezuela where these sectors constituted a majority of the population.

In the English-speaking Caribbean, the white colonizers continued to form the dominant elite, although a middle sector emerged, composed of whites, together with Lebanese, Chinese, and other immigrant ethnic groups and those mulattoes who were able, by way of the educational system, to occupy administrative posts and thus improve their social status. However, the situation of the black majority changed very little. As a result of the nationalist movements of the 1930s, the British government was obliged to increase local political participation, enabling a middle strata of mulattoes to form part of the political elite and become leaders of the black population. Nevertheless, the gradual nature of the decolonization process impeded the development of a massive, militant base for the proposed political autonomy of this emerging political elite.

The East Indian population was brought to Guyana and Trinidad and Tobago as a work force to compensate for labor shortages generated by the abolition of slavery. Initially submerged into the subordinate sector of society, the East Indians began to enter the middle sectors as their indentured servant contracts expired and, later on, even managed to form part of the economic elites.

With political independence, the social and racial structure of the English-speaking Caribbean changed. The new elites were predominantly mulattoes and, to a lesser extent, blacks. Nevertheless, in some cases such as Barbados, the economic elite continued to be predominantly white. In Guyana and Trinidad and Tobago, as a result of the division of these societies between sharply separated racial and ethnic groups, the elites and the middle sectors also contained mulattoes, blacks, and East Indians, while the subordinate sectors were predominantly black and East Indian.

At present, both in Latin America and in the English-speaking Caribbean, the situation has changed very little. In countries with a large Amerindian population, such as Mexico, Peru, Bolivia, and Ecuador, among others, Amerindians generally have a subordinate status, together with the blacks in those countries. The mestizos and mulattoes also form part of this sector, although some have risen to the middle sectors. At the same time, the elites are predominantly made up of whites, mestizos, and mulattoes. In societies such as Venezuela, Colombia, and Brazil, where the Amerindian population is a clear minority, it is for the most part isolated, not only socially but also geographically, and is concentrated principally in the border zones.

In the English-speaking Caribbean, although blacks generally represent more than one-half of the total population, they are largely confined to the subordinate sectors. The mulatto groups, some blacks, and the small white population make up the dominant class, which is generally divided between a black and mulatto political elite and a white and mulatto economic elite. In Guyana and Trinidad and Tobago, the economic elite also includes East Indians.

This racial and ethnic diversity of the social structure in the different countries of these regions has led the political elites, when convenient, to use different ethnic and racial strategies[4] to forge, develop, and consolidate national identities and political movements.[5] This has meant that the use of racial and ethnic elements in ideological[6] and political discourse, whether on the part of the elites or the subordinate sectors, has been intimately related to the particular ethnic and racial characteristics of these societies. The changing morphology of interethnic relations in each of the regions has been reflected in the greater or lesser emphasis placed on ethnic and racial themes within specific political movements and in their ideological use by the dominant sectors.

Latin America

"Indigenista" Ideologies and Integrationist Policies

Since the 1930s, the political and economic elites of various Latin American countries have sought a means to activate and modernize their economies in order to participate fully in the prospects of capitalist development. To this end, the incorporation of the Amerindian population into the labor force was regarded as imperative. Thus, in Mexico, for example, agrarian reform led to the transformation of the Amerindians and mestizos into peasants by way of dividing existing communities and by the dissolution of community traditions.

In those Latin American countries with an Amerindian population, whether large or small, the 1940s witnessed the state's development and use of an "indigenista" ideology, which emerged initially in Mexico and was conceived as a justification for the integration of the Amerindian and mestizo populations into national society. This ideology was based on the so-called "theory of internal colonialism,"[7] which asserted the need to integrate the different ethnic groups into national culture in order to eliminate cultural dualism and thus contribute to overcoming the "underdevelopment" and "backwardness" that characterized these countries.

In terms of national identities and political projects, this integration policy was justified by arguing that the Amerindian cultures were stagnant and backward and that, therefore, it was necessary to "civilize" the Amerindians and incorporate them into modern society. It was also argued that diverse ethnic identities should not exist alongside the national society, that they were mere remnants of "backwardness" and "underdevelopment." In consequence, it was imperative to promote a national identity devoid of pluralistic elements, apart from the possible inclusion of ethnic elements to nurture folklore. At the same time, this process of social integration and cultural assimilation was important for the development of the political aspirations of the governing elites (especially in those countries with large Amerindian and mestizo populations), because they needed to guarantee the support of these sectors for the populist projects that they normally pursued.

Later on, as a result of the influence of theoretical approaches related to Third World positions and a preoccupation for "the free determination of peoples," a new tendency emerged within the "indigenista" school that defended ethnic and racial pluralism. Thus, the so-called "new indigenismo" was born, identified with progressive positions and regarded as the liberal wing of the "indigenista" movement. It criticized the capitalist modernization promoted by the governing elites, arguing that the traditional forms of organization, characteristic of the Amerindian communities, were generally superior. They therefore advocated the defense of Amerindian interests, assuming proposals of so-called critical anthropology and ethnopopulism.[8] This position, although it initially challenged state policy, was eventually absorbed into the state structure in the 1960s and 1970s.

Thus, the political discourse adopted by the elites included the need to promote self-government, bilingualism, and ethnic and racial pluralism in the Amerindian zones, independently of the size of the territories involved. The basic concern was still to preserve their political and cultural hegemony. They reacted more or less in the same way when, as in earlier periods, they had accepted the incorporation of the Amerindian as an integral part of national identity and its symbolism. Frequently, the introduction of these new "indigenista" conceptions responded as much to pressure from local Amerindian communities as to the creation of an international movement in defense of the Amerindian minorities. However, in the 1970s, in those Latin American societies where military regimes took power (as, for example, in Chile, Brazil, and Argentina), such notions were rapidly banned.

The "Indianista" Movement

The Cuban Revolution, the new Third World perspectives, and the struggle for the free determination of nations were also to influence the subordinate sectors in Latin America. In the case of the Amerindian population, two important movements emerged toward the end of the 1960s and in the 1970s. First, the "Indianista" movement was promoted by Amerindian leaders who advocated the need to struggle to defend their ethnic and racial roots, using some of the ideas offered by the new "indigenismo." Second, another movement was inspired by Marxist theory. It argued that the Amerindian population was affected profoundly by class problems and that, as a result, it ought to participate in class organizations and ignore ethnic differences. In this way, they offered a "class" version of the integrationist position.

The "Indianistas," for their part, endeavored to recover their ancestral lands and achieve self-government. Their arguments were based on the need to strengthen ethnic identities and traditional organizational structures in order to resist the integrationist and acculturation policies of the dominant sectors. In this sense, they coincided with some of the positions suggested by the new "indigenismo." The representatives of the Marxist tendency, however, maintained that the Amerindian population should be included in the political projects of the dominated classes by virtue of the fact that they already formed part of these classes as a result of the process of proletarianization or of subjection to mercantile productive relations.

These two positions represented the extremes in relation to the ethnic question. One emphasized it; the other ignored it. The former naturally opted for a discourse which, as in the case of official "indigenismo," underlined the importance of ethnic and racial ingredients.

The "Invisibility" of the Blacks

Latin American societies with appreciable black populations largely ignored blacks in the formulation of national political projects. Such populations suffered from what has been referred to as a process of social "invisibility."[9] The African-descended population and its cultural heritage simply were not considered relevant in the forging of a national identity, either by the political and economic elites or by the majority of intellectuals.[10] It was regarded as necessary, as in the case of the Amerindian population, to introduce blacks to "civilization" to maintain the cultural hegemony of the white elites. African roots were considered pagan, exotic, and savage, thus incapable of contributing to the formation of a Latin American national identity. Whereas the Amerindian was accepted, in some cases, as an important element in the national ideology proposed by the emerging elites, blacks were completely excluded.

The depersonalization of blacks in Latin American societies has its historical explanation in the violent deculturalization and assimilation to which they were submitted when they arrived in the New World as slaves. They faced the alternative of trying to recover an identity that had been separated from its original cultural roots or of accepting what the dominant elite was determined to impose. In these circumstances, the cultural elements typical of the black population could not be reproduced or projected at a national level. African culture survived only in reduced pockets of cultural resistance, as in magic and religious traditions.

In the Dominican Republic, forging a national identity while ignoring the contribution of black and African elements led Dominican blacks and mulattoes to identify themselves as "indigenous" in order to differentiate themselves from the Haitian blacks. This distinction between Dominican and Haitian blacks was seen as particularly important as a result of the political problems between the two nations.[11] The particular political status of Puerto Rico transformed it into a special case. Beyond generally ignoring blacks as a Puerto Rican national identity was forged, North American racism was a predominant influence and, despite an official policy that was formally anti-racist, assumed proportions unequaled in the rest of Latin America.[12]

Puerto Rico's status as a "freely associated state" makes it difficult to affirm the existence of a national identity or a national political ethos because the interests of the elites are much more closely identified with and controlled by the United States than in the rest of Latin America. Furthermore, while the Puerto Rican independence movement has embraced symbols inherited from its Spanish tradition in order to confront North American influence, it has not incorporated black ethnic or racial themes into its discourse.[13]

The Black Population in Brazil

The Brazilian case is particularly interesting. Official policy is opposed to racism and racial discrimination, but, in practice, blacks have been discriminated against economically, politically, and socially. Furthermore, attempts to study this situation have been opposed in official circles to the extent that in 1969, during the military regime, studies that documented racial discrimination were prohibited.[14]

Particularly during Brazil's military dictatorship, the movements that attempted to revitalize black ethnic identity were characterized as subversive and were repressed in the name of "national security." During the 1970s, this tendency was associated with the prevalence of an official ideology that postulated the existence of a "racial democracy," such as that proposed by Gilberto Freyre in the 1930s. As in the case of "indigenismo," the underlying assumption was that if blacks were found predominantly in the lower strata of the society, this was the result of "backwardness" rooted in their slave heritage,[15] which could be ameliorated through the process of cultural assimilation.

In those Latin American countries with a black population, projects based on racial and ethnic considerations had little impact among the subordinate sectors. In general, Black Power had little influence, except in countries such as Brazil[16] where, despite the military repression, a "Black-Río" or "Brazil-Soul" movement emerged among the youth of the poor urban sectors of Rio de Janeiro. The movement spread to other large Brazilian cities, especially in intellectual and university circles. The movement sought to exalt black identity while fluctuating between cultural and political definitions.

The official sector, which was still identified with the "racial democracy" thesis, reacted as expected, accusing anyone who assumed positions similar to those of Black Power of promoting a black nationalism that called into question the very basis of Brazilian national identity. This was seen as "unBrazilian." In the same way, the dominant elites criticized the discourse that exalted black values because to them it represented a form of North American intervention and the acceptance of foreign cultural norms that would undermine national culture. However, the movement itself, which was basically cultural and primarily musical, soon became commercialized and eventually contributed little to the development of a black ethnic identity or to autonomous political movements.

More recently, the so-called "democratic opening" permitted the founding of new political parties and organizations, including some with a clear ethnic identification. One of these, the "Unified Black Movement against Racial Discrimination," once again took up the idea that Brazilian society needed radical changes in order to achieve an authentic racial democracy, more substantial than that proposed by the elites. In this way, the members of the movement have combined their ethnic and racial propositions with economic, political, and social demands.

In sum, in Latin America throughout the entire national period, the dominant sectors have aimed at orienting, acculturating, integrating, and assimilating the non-white sectors into a national society while consolidating their own cultural hegemony. At most, they have conceded the symbolic incorporation of some Amerindian and, to a much lesser extent, African-American elements. Within this context, national identity has been conceived as a process of forging ethnic and cultural uniformity by way of a discourse that, in general, excludes any ethnic or racial commentary. The objective is a homogeneous identity, occasionally identified as "mestizo," but frequently assumed, at least implicitly, to be European.

The English-speaking Caribbean

Nationalist Ideology: Decolonization and the Independence Movements

In the greater part of the English-speaking Caribbean, after the Second World War, ethnic and racial minorities (basically mulattoes, East Indians, Chinese, and others) began to be incorporated into the higher social spheres of society and, in particular, into the economic elites. Increased educational opportunities, an expanded civil service, and accelerated urbanization enabled the black population to begin to ascend to middle-sector status. Nevertheless, by virtue of their numbers, blacks also made up the vast majority of the subordinate sector.

With the end of the colonial era, national ideology as expressed by the emerging political elites downplayed ethnic, racial, and social differences in order to unify the local population. (Guyana and Trinidad and Tobago were exceptions to this trend.) The decolonization process, led by predominantly mulatto middle sectors seeking political power, limited the objective to political independence negotiated on the basis of gradual concessions by the colonial power, without promoting militant mass support nor the radical politicization of the subordinate sectors.[17] At the same time, despite the prevalence of a nationalist ideology, these elites were influenced profoundly by colonial culture. This became clear when their notion of national identity and political organization reflected the ideologies and political structures of the metropolis.

In general, the emerging political elites based their political movements on the need for multiracial and pluralist alliances that would permit the building of these new nations. Just as in Latin America, national development presupposed an integration and uniformity of society that, in turn, required the acceptance of the national identity and the political objectives proposed by these elites. Such nationalist ideology, although largely rhetorical, also served to confront alternative political movements whose discourse combined ethnic, racial, and class components that could eventually threaten the status quo.

Later on, in cases such as the People's National Party (PNP) in Jamaica or the New Jewel Movement in Grenada, nationalist objectives were emphasized, suggesting that "national" interests were being threatened by the hegemonic presence of the United States. In these cases, it was once again necessary to achieve national unity beyond ethnic, racial, and social differences in order to develop movements that promised authentic economic and political independence, although they also included an emphasis on the Afro-Caribbean identity.

As a response to this nationalist ideology, two alternative types of ideological discourse emerged in the late 1960s and the 1970s: the first, fundamentally ethnoracial, was influenced by Black Power and the revival of the Rastafarian movement; the second was a discourse based on Marxist conceptions. In some cases, such as the so-called "Caribbean socialism" and some of the more radical socialist positions, we find a combination of elements drawn from Marxist thought with others influenced by ethnoracial ideology.[18]

Ethnoracial Ideology: Black Power and the Rastafarian Movement

The existence of a predominantly black subordinate sector in the English-speaking Caribbean led to the emergence in different historical moments of movements, such as Rastafarianism, that extolled black and

African values. However, at the outset of the 1960s, these movements adopted a perspective oriented more toward Third World positions. Such was the case of the Rastafarian movement that emphasized the anti-white and anti-metropolitan sentiment of the subjugated black population.[19] In the English-speaking Caribbean, unlike in Latin America, the impact of movements that projected ethnic and racial factors assumed a certain importance. The Rastafarian movement, which emerged initially in Jamaica and achieved some influence in Trinidad and Tobago, Dominica, Antigua, Grenada, and St. Lucia, was an example of the ideological alternatives that combined ethnic, racial, and political elements.[20]

High unemployment and underemployment in the late 1960s and the 1970s, together with increasing poverty among the majority of the population, encouraged militancy in movements inspired by the Black Power movement. Rastafarians were embraced as part of this movement by the popular sectors and especially by unemployed urban youth. As a result, political and intellectual elites who occasionally provided these sectors with leadership incorporated ethnic and racial demands into their discourse. The Afro-Caribbean identity progressively was regarded as more appropriate than the Anglo-Saxon identity that had characterized post-war nationalist leadership.

Black Power, originally inspired by the ideals of Caribbean authors such as Marcus Garvey, exercised a clear influence on the movements that intellectual groups were developing in the English-speaking Caribbean during the 1960s and 1970s. In the initial stages, the movements concentrated on ethnic and racial themes, emphasizing the need to recover and strengthen African and black origins of the majority of the population. Nevertheless, with few exceptions, such as Jamaica, this ideology of black supremacy provoked little positive response among the black majorities who continued to support the pluriclass and multiracial policies of the major parties. Later on, under the influence of Walter Rodney of Guyana and other intellectuals, and as a result of the politically progressive processes in Jamaica, Grenada, and Guyana, ethnic and racial themes began to be included in the debate on class and national issues.

In this way, at the political level, new groups and movements led by intellectuals attempted to combine an ethnically rooted nationalism with anti-imperialism and nondogmatic Marxism. At this point, what came to be known as "Caribbean socialism" began to emerge. It extolled the black roots that were emphasized by ethnoracial ideology as the basis for the development of an authentic Caribbean national identity.[21] Undoubtedly, these new groups made an important contribution to the forging of national identities more closely linked to the ethnic and racial origins of their societies. The objective was to break with the dominant metropolitan ideology. Walter Rodney, for example, emphasized the need for a "cultural reconstruction" in order to undermine the cultural hegemony of the elites by reviving the African cultural roots of the majority of the black Caribbean population.[22]

Black intellectuals argued that, despite the fact that in some of these societies the political and economic elites were mulatto and in other cases black, they did not respond to the interests of the masses because they had been culturally colonized. These elites were regarded as allies of European and North American white power, and as a result, the development of a pro-black, nationalist policy was considered absolutely necessary. Some of the resulting movements, such as the New Jewel Movement in Grenada, came to be identified with more radical or revolutionary alternatives, in contrast to the more reformist tendencies within "Caribbean socialism."

Despite the apparent success of the New Jewel Movement in the late 1970s and early 1980s, by the late 1970s ethnic and racial elements were being downplayed in the discourse of those political elites who had previously adopted them in order to consolidate their hegemony. With the growing foreign debt and a continuing fall in the prices of the main export products, new problems began to demand increasing attention. Once again, emphasis had to be placed on a national unity that sought to transcend ethnic, racial, and class interests, although without abandoning a marked preference for the African component at the expense of other ethnic elements, such as the East Indian or Amerindian.

During the 1960s and 1970s, in the CARICOM countries, as in Latin America, internal and external factors led to the development of an opposition that promoted ethnic and racial elements and sought to present an alternative to the political parties promoted by the economic and political elites. Parties and movements inspired by ideologies emphasizing ethnoracial elements underlined the need to recreate and revive ethnic and racial factors. In contrast, the movements and parties inspired by Marxist ideology, although occasionally recognizing the need to incorporate ethnic and racial demands, clearly emphasized class relations.

Ethnic Polarization in Guyana and Trinidad and Tobago

Unlike the other English-speaking Caribbean countries, in Guyana and Trinidad and Tobago, ethnic and racial differences have produced persistent divisions of society. In both countries, it is difficult to identify a single national identity. In Guyana, for example, initially Indo-Guyanese and Afro-Guyanese participated jointly in an anticolonial front that later broke apart for ideological reasons and eventually led to ethnic polarization.[23] In Trinidad and Tobago, there was a similar process, so that even now differences among the political parties have a marked ethnic and racial connotation.

Ethnic polarization[24] was, to a great degree, a result of the extremely rapid acculturation of blacks (as was the case in Latin America), while the East Indians preserved their distinctive cultural, linguistic, religious, and social norms. Ethnic identification, in opposition to the "others," was used by political elites in each of the ethnic groups to preserve their hegemony within the group itself. The basic concern was inter-elite rivalry for access to postcolonial economic and political power. In both countries, despite the nationalist rhetoric, what emerged were political movements that, despite their ideological differences, used racial and ethnic arguments in order to consolidate popular support among the different ethnic groups. This type of politics downplayed class distinctions, emphasized racial and ethnic differences, and consolidated divisions along these lines.

Conclusions

The impact of racial and ethnic factors and their influences on national identities and the political movements of the dominant elites have developed somewhat differently in Latin America and the English-speaking Caribbean. In the Latin American countries, national characteristics were able to take root over a longer period of time. This allowed for the development of "integrationist policies" that incorporated the majority of the different social sectors by means of political movements and ideological arguments that were constantly renewed. Consequently, it proved more difficult merely to emphasize racial or ethnic factors in national political debate. In some countries, such as Mexico, the political importance of mestizo sectors gave rise to the symbolic incorporation of Amerindian elements into national identity, together with assimilative policies such as "indigenismo."

The process was different in the more recently politically independent English-speaking Caribbean countries that have had much less time to develop and consolidate their respective national identities. Precisely because national identities were not altogether consolidated, proposals expressed in ethnic and racial demands, as in the case of Black Power, had more receptive populations.

Furthermore, the nature of the break with the colonial past also exercised different influences. Throughout Latin America, radical and violent struggles for independence helped to consolidate national identities relatively rapidly. In the English-speaking Caribbean, the gradual decolonization process was accompanied by a retention of the social and political systems inherited from the metropolitan power. In these countries, there was less pressure to emphasize national identity. We have also seen that the emerging elites, beyond the nationalist rhetoric of the postindependence era, were profoundly identified with the metropolis. In fact, the struggle for independence did not impede the continued influence of the colonizing country, clearly evidenced in the persistence of the cultural, political, and social legacy of the preindependence period. It was only after the achievement of political independence that a cultural nationalism emerged, advocating national identities based partly on the need to rediscover the African heritage and to consolidate the black and mulatto elites.

In Latin America, national identities and patriotic political movements originally were based on the idea that the fundamental problem was how to confront the former colonizers after independence had been achieved. As a result, great emphasis was placed on the building of a nation-state whose consolidation required limiting demands of a social, ethnic, or racial nature. In some countries, such as Peru and Mexico, the Amerindian legacy was incorporated into the populist and nationalist discourse, while in countries with a small Amerindian population, such as Venezuela, this element was excluded. Another important difference is that the contribution of the black population to national identity and the associated projects, if not totally absent, was extremely reduced. References to black or African traditions were largely absent from the discourse engaged in by economic and political elites that were made up predominantly of whites, mulattoes, and mestizos. This historical legacy of ignoring the black population during the formation of national identities has contributed to some negative perceptions.[25] The English-speaking Caribbean countries consider that, while they have a positive attitude toward their black populations, in Latin America there is a "structural racism" that keeps black citizens subjected to lower economic, political, and social status.[26]

The actual situation is that racial prejudice exists in both regions: in Latin America, against Amerindians and blacks; in the English-speaking Caribbean, basically against the white, Amerindian, and East Indian communities. Consequently, the problem of internal racism in these societies needs to be analyzed, taking into account the diverse ethnic and socioeconomic characteristics of the elites who acceded to power in the postcolonial period and their use of the "ethnic card" in the formation of their respective national identities.

In the Caribbean, greater importance and power have been attached to ethnic and racial factors than in Latin America. Indeed, in certain historical moments, these factors became an important unifying force that overshadowed economic, political, and social considerations. This was particularly so in the late 1960s and 1970s when emphasis on an Afro-Caribbean identity was at its height. By way of contrast, and with few exceptions, in Latin America ethnic and racial factors have been of secondary importance in affirming national identity.

Currently, in both Latin America and the Caribbean, it appears that the dominant elites will tend to reinforce policies favoring ethnic and racial integration. Collaboration, social peace, and national unity are defined as the main objectives. However, with increases in the poverty index, the economic, social, and political exclusion of the subordinate sectors is increasingly evident. In this situation, it is clear that either "mainstream" or "alternative" political movements that refuse to contemplate ethnic and racial pluralism will continue to reproduce the discrimination and racism present in these societies.

Notes

1. For a detailed analysis of this process and its consequences, see Rex 1978, 9-49.

2. Serbin 1988, 40-54.

3. For an analysis of the historical development of the miscegenation and acculturization processes of these sectors and their relation to the process of assimilation into the emerging Latin American societies, see Morner 1969.

4. "Ethnic" factors refer to those cultural and social elements shared by a given human group, while "racial" factors are based on the hereditary phenotypical characteristics of such groups. For a more extensive discussion of these concepts, see Serbin 1987 and the extensive bibliography on the theme in the same book; Morner 1969; Fennema and Lowenthal 1987; and Enloe 1973.

5. By "national identity," we understand those collective representations, conscious or unconscious, that accompany an identification with a particular nation-state and that, in consequence, differentiate its members from those of other nation-states. It is composed of cultural, linguistic, social, and psychological elements that give its members the sense of belonging to a collectivity while, at the same time, guaranteeing the permanence and continuity of the nation-state. See Bonfil Batalla 1987; Serbin 1988 and the bibliography quoted by this author; and Colombres 1988. By "political projects," we understand the programs developed by political parties or movements in order to further their objectives. Based on a particular vision of the world and of society, they are translated into goals and expressed in strategies designed to achieve them. As a result, political projects will have a theoretical or doctrinal basis and a specific political *praxis* related to the interests of certain social groups.

6. By "ideologies," we understand the ideas, values, and representations present in political discourse, both of the elites and of the subordinate sectors. In the sense suggested by Antonio Gramsci, they are intimately linked to the search for and the exercise of hegemony within society. Thus, in each and every case, the objective is the creation of a consensus in society that would make a particular political project dominant, using ideologies as vehicles for the development and consolidation of this hegemony over other social sectors by means of a consensual process. By "hegemony," we understand the utilization, by a given social class, of instruments and mechanisms that permit the achievement of this consensus and, as a result, the support of other social sectors for its own, particular project. In the same way, the incorporation and utilization at the level of discourse of ideas and representations related to ethnic, racial, or social differences within the society in order to gain or maintain hegemony will be considered "interpellations" or "referents." See Serbin 1988 and the extensive bibliography he quotes; Enloe 1973; and Colombres 1988.

7. Hegg 1982, 235-236. For a more extensive analysis of the "indigenista" policies implemented in Latin America, consult Bartra 1978, 427; Stavenhagen 1988; *Latin American Perspectives* IX (2), 1982; and Colombres 1988.

8. Díaz-Polanco 1988, 35-39.

9. de Friedemann 1984, 510-562.

10. With the exception of some social scientists and writers, among whom we can name Miguel Acosta Saignes, Nina de Friedemann, Alejo Carpentier, and Moreno Fraginals. Nevertheless, there are some attempts to overcome this situation; among others, and in the case of Venezuela, consult Ramos Guédez 1985; *Black Latin America* 1977, which offers an extensive bibliography on the theme for Latin America and the Caribbean.

11. An extensive discussion of this point can be found in Fennema and Lowenthal 1987, which also analyzes the racial elements in the discourse of Dominican President Joaquín Balaguer. See also Toletino 1974; and Fundación Cultural Dominicana 1973.

12. This relationship meant that the "dream of being white" was much more strongly rooted among the Puerto Ricans. See Segrera 1973.

13. Segrera 1973, 119-122.

14. Fontaine 1985, 2. On the theme of racial inequality and discrimination, see also Hasenbalg 1979.

15. Skidmore 1979, 12.

16. For more details, see Turner 1979; Fontaine 1979; Mitchell 1979; and González 1979.

17. Sankatsing 1989, 24.

18. Serbin 1988, 404-405; see also Benn 1987, which offers an extensive analysis of the different political ideologies in the English-speaking Caribbean.

19. Serbin 1988, 273.

20. Yawney 1976 offers a complete study of this point in relation to the Rastafarians.

21. Serbin 1988, 358.

22. Serbin 1988, 386.

23. For a detailed analysis of the Guyana case, see Serbin 1979.

24. M.G. Smith first discussed this problem, adapting Furnivall's idea of cultural pluralism to the Caribbean. Smith argued that, despite ethnic and racial differences, all these groups made up a society for the simple reason that they shared a common government system. In this way, as in the case of "indigenismo" and the Afro-American population in Latin America, national identity was conceived of as above and beyond

any ethnic identities. The existence of cultural and institutional differences was recognized, but power was exercised by one of the cultural groups that made up the society, although the attempt to guarantee harmonious relations was not always achieved. Thus, the governments assumed the role of regulating any possible interethnic conflicts and were responsible for trying to preserve political and economic stability in these countries. For more details, see Serbin 1979, 70.

25. Serbin 1988b, 16-19.

26. Manigat 1988, 344-356.

References

Bartra, Roger. 1978. "El problema indígena y la política indigenista." In *Raza y clase en la sociedad postcolonial.* Paris: UNESCO.

Benn, Denis. 1987. *The Growth and Development of Political Ideas in the Caribbean: 1774-1983.* Mona, Jamaica: Institute of Social and Economic Research, University of the West Indies.

Black Latin America. 1977. Latin American Bibliographical Series No. 5. Los Angeles: Latin American Studies Center, California State University.

Bonfil Batalla, Guillermo. 1987. "La teoría del control cultural en el estudio de procesos étnicos." *Revista Papeles de la Casa Chata* 2 (3).

Colombres, Adolfo. 1988. *La hora del bárbaro.* Third edition. Buenos Aires: Ediciones del Sol.

de Friedemann, Nina S. 1984. "Estudios de negros en la antropología colombiana." In *Un siglo de investigación.* Bogotá.

Díaz-Polanco, Hector. 1988. *La cuestión étnico-nacional.* Second edition. Mexico: Editorial Fontamara.

Enloe, Cynthia. 1973. *Ethnic Conflict and Political Development.* Boston: Little, Brown and Company.

Fennema, Miendert, and Troetje Lowenthal. 1987. *Construcción de raza y nación en República Dominicana.* Santo Domingo: Editorial Universitaria-Universidad Autónoma de Santo Domingo.

Fontaine, Pierre-Michel, ed. 1985. *Race, Class and Power in Brazil.* Los Angeles: Center for African Studies, University of California.

Fontaine, Pierre-Michel. 1985. "Blacks and the Search for Power in Brazil." In *Race, Class and Power in Brazil,* ed. Pierre-Michel Fontaine. Los Angeles: Center for African Studies, University of California.

Fundación Cultural Dominicana, Museo del Hombre Dominicano. 1973. *Ensayos sobre cultura dominicana.* Second edition. Santo Domingo: Editorial Edil, Río Piedras.

Giacalone, Rita, ed. 1988. *Estudios del Caribe en Venezuela.* Caracas: Fondo Acta Científica Venezuela y Consejo de Desarrollo Científico y Humanístico.

González, Lelia. 1985. "The Unified Black Movement." In *Race, Class and Power in Brazil,* ed. Pierre-Michel Fontaine. Los Angeles: Center for African Studies, University of California.

Hasenbalg, Carlos A. 1979. *Discriminaçao e desigualdades raçais no Brasil.* Rio de Janeiro: Ediçoes Graal.

Hegg, Ortega. 1982. "El conflicto étnia-nación en Nicaragua." In *América Latina: Etnodesarrollo y etnocidio.* San José, Costa Rica: FLACSO.

Henry, Francis, ed. 1976. *Ethnicity in the Americas.* La Haya.

Latin American Perspectives. 1982. "Minorities in the Americas," IX (2).

Manigat, Leslie. 1988. "The Caribbean between Global Horizons and Latin American Perspectives." In *The Caribbean and World Politics*. New York: Holmes & Meier.

Mitchell, Michael. 1985. "Blacks and the 'abertura democrática'." In *Race, Class and Power in Brazil*, ed. Pierre-Michel Fontaine. Los Angeles: Center for African Studies, University of California.

Morner, Magnus. 1969. *La mezcla de razas en la historia de América Latina*. Buenos Aires: Editorial Paidos.

Ramos Guédez, José Marcial. 1985. *El negro en Venezuela: Aporte bibliográfico*. Second edition. Caracas: Instituto Autónomo Biblioteca Nacional y de Servicios de Bibliotecas, Gobernación del Estado Miranda.

Rex, John. 1978. "Introducción: Las nuevas naciones y las minorías étnicas, aspectos teóricos y comparados." In *Raza y clase en la sociedad postcolonial*. Paris: UNESCO.

Sankatsing, Glenn. 1989. *Caribbean Social Science*. An Assessment. Caracas: URSHLAC-UNESCO.

Segrera, Martín. 1973. *Racismo y política en Puerto Rico*. Río Piedras: Editorial Edil.

Serbin, Andrés. 1979. *Nacionalismo, etnicidad y política en la República Cooperativa de Guyana*. Caracas: Editorial Bruguera.

Serbin, Andrés. 1987. *Etnicidad, clase y nación en el Caribe de habla inglesa*. Caracas: Biblioteca de la Academia Nacional de Historia.

Serbin, Andrés. 1988a. "Identidad cultural y desarrollo en el Caribe anglófono: Algunas reflexiones desde una visión antropológica." *Revue du CERC (Centre d'Etudes et de Recherches Caraibeenes)* 5. Guadeloupe: Université des Antilles-Guyane.

Skidmore, Thomas. 1985. "Race and Class in Brazil: Historical Perspectives." In *Race, Class and Power in Brazil*, ed. Pierre-Michel Fontaine. Los Angeles: Center for African Studies, University of California.

Stavenhagen, Rodolfo. 1988. *Derecho indígena y derechos humanos en América Latina*. Mexico: Instituto Interamericano de Derechos Humanos and El Colegio de México.

Toletino, Hugo. 1974. *Razas e historia en Santo Domingo*. Santo Domingo: Editora de la Universidad Autónoma de Santo Domingo.

Turner, J. Michael. 1985. "Brown into Black: Changing Racial Attitudes of Afro-Brazilian Students." In *Race, Class and Power in Brazil*, ed. Pierre-Michel Fontaine. Los Angeles: Center for African Studies, University of California.

Yawney, C.D. 1976. "Remnants of all Nations: Rastafarian Attitudes to Race and Nationality." In *Ethnicity in the Americas*, ed. Francis Henry. La Haya.

Chapter Four

Images of the "Other":
Caribbean Society Through the Eyes of
Cuban and West Indian Writers

Lulú Giménez Saldivia

This study is a preliminary review of Latin American and Caribbean images of each other. It analyzes literary images with a view to appreciating what the groups know of each other, how they relate to each other, and the ways in which they evaluate each other.

A review of the literary contributions of all the countries in the two regions would require a far more extensive and ambitious research project. We have opted to limit our coverage, using geographical criteria. We will examine the West Indies and the Spanish-speaking Caribbean, in both cases analyzing essays, prose, and poetry. While the West Indies does not possess strictly "national" literatures, each of the Latin American countries has accumulated a *corpus* of literary works that responds to a particular local dynamic. As a result, any work written in one of the English-speaking countries may be regarded as potentially representative of the entire group, but the same cannot be said for Latin America.

In order to capture the tendencies of prevailing perceptions and of the images derived from them, various historical essays have been reviewed that reveal the ways in which stereotypes of the "other" have been formed. This is an indispensable starting point in order to understand the role of colonial ideology in the respective perceptions that have been conveyed through succeeding generations.

On the basis of an initial identification of the fundamental ideological notions that contribute to the images of "otherness," we will recognize three readings of the perceptive images to be found in the analyzed texts. The intention of this study is to cover the three basic dimensions of perception, according to the scheme proposed by Tzvetan Todorov.[1] These dimensions are the axiological, the praxeological, and the epistemological and embrace the basic modalities of interaction between two realities.

General Considerations

L atin America and the English-speaking Caribbean constitute two supranational groupings that have come only recently into contact and that traditionally have been characterized by a mutual ignorance. The image of the "other," the unknown, has turned on a series of judgments, generally based on stereotypes and prejudices. These judgments naturally have conditioned the first systematic relations between the two groupings, and these in turn have been stimulated by geopolitical changes. To the extent that contacts have become closer and more generalized, we can also distinguish other types of mutual perceptions that could mean a significant advance toward stable ties on the basis of mutual respect.

In general, we can affirm that, in the literary corpus in question, there is no structured imagery in relation to the other group, as a specific ontological reality. Very few authors have attempted to construct literary images that reflect the physical or cultural presence of Latin America in the English-speaking Caribbean countries, or of the West Indies in Latin America. Furthermore, existing images refer, in the majority of cases, neither to Latin America nor to the English-speaking Caribbean as abstract entities, but rather to concrete elements that serve as points of contact between the cultures of the respective groups of countries. Some of these elements derive from the geographical contiguity and migratory flows in the area. However, apart from these isolated examples, we can conclude that the images of the Latin American world do not "speak" to Caribbean intellectuals and vice versa.

So we can conclude that, despite the existence of certain common features in the respective popular cultures — for example, the Christmas "parrandas" in Trinidad and Tobago and certain other traditions among rural Trinidadians of Hispanic descent — these have not transcended adequately in literary imagery.

There are many reasons for this lack of structured imagery. In the first place, the colonizing ideologies have prevented the "appropriation" by these cultures of symbols that are alien to the thought structures and visions of the world inherited from the respective metropolitan colonizers. For a long time, the two groups of countries were isolated from one another and characterized by a mutual lack of understanding and indifference. That was precisely the impression registered by Vidiadhar Surajprasad (V.S.) Naipaul, who, during the course of his life in Trinidad, had only a vague idea of the existence of a distant continent that did not figure in formal British educational texts. In *Finding the Center*, an attempt to write his autobiography, Naipaul comments, "Trinidad was small, an island, a British colony. The maps in our geography books, concentrating on the British islands in the Caribbean, seemed to stress our smallness and isolation. In the map of Trinidad, the map which I grew to carry in my head, Venezuela was an unexplained little peninsula in the top lefthand corner."[2]

In the second place, both Caribbean and Latin American literatures have been impregnated, during a prolonged period, by Eurocentric models that made it extremely difficult to incorporate elements from popular culture into literary themes. Furthermore, in these countries writers come from a restricted social strata and generally have their expectations defined in terms of the large European editorials. The public the writer has in mind is made up of anonymous readers, thus provoking a nervous quest for universalism, for which particular, local experiences might constitute negatives. In the English-speaking Caribbean, this tendency was aggravated, on the one hand, by the high illiteracy rate that constituted an insurmountable barrier between the writer and his society and, on the other, by the small collective size of these countries within the general context of the English-speaking public: "Writers have received greater recognition outside the Caribbean than within it.... The importance of a writer depends on the British publishing houses. For what could be called the 'commercialization of culture,' the Caribbean market is too small."[3]

In the third place, and more recently, both literatures have assumed a way of understanding "cultural identity" that has led them to stress those elements that differentiate their respective cultural heritages from others, even those closest at hand, obviating elements they could have in common. In this sense, "miscegenation," "syncretism," "Latinism," and "Afro-Antilleanism" have been converted into categories that define cultural forms and contents assumed by the literature of the region as a contribution to the search for its cultural identity. Thus, in Latin America an important part of literary activity has been oriented toward the affirmation of a Latin America with its own personality — defined as a continent that is both mestizo and universalist but always insisting on the Latin strain, which is precisely what opens up its universalist pretensions. In contrast, literature in the English-speaking Caribbean, during an important stage in its development, was trapped within the dichotomy between Europe and Africa, with its corresponding synthesis, and totally indifferent to Hispanic America. In short, both experiences basically sought to legitimize their own cultures, which, in the eyes of the world — or of the Europeans who had coined the very idea of universality — had become bogged down in the obscurity of the New World.

Since the 1960s, this situation has undergone a qualitative change, prompted by continental geopolitical factors. As a result, we can now distinguish a literature which, in each of the two regions, proves that there is a new interest in exploring the characteristics that the respective cultural formations have in common, a literature that is open to the incorporation of new and novel elements offered by local and neighboring experiences. Nevertheless, as we are referring to a very recent change, it must be understood that it has emerged slowly. It is, therefore, initially impossible to decide if we are in the presence of an irreversible process that augurs closer links and greater integration or of a mere option that emerges in this particular moment as a result of conjunctural circumstances and is, therefore, subject to the way the winds of change continue to blow.

In any event, one of the reasons for emphasizing these aspects of the problem is to suggest the limitations of literature as a source for the study of mutual images. Thus, the images that can be captured and that may well reflect the way in which the "other" is seen, cannot be taken as hard evidence; they need to be compared with the contribution of other cultural and social experiences, among them, those offered by oral tradition and other expressions of popular culture.

Colonized Perception:
Some Comments on the Formation of Stereotypes

For a long time, the Caribbean did not exist as a specific ontological reality because its entire system of symbolic references was organized by the respective colonial metropolis and responded to European epistemological and valuative models. During this period, the only common point of reference for the English-speaking Caribbean was the United Kingdom and those neighboring English-speaking countries in a similar situation. The rest of the world was seen through English eyes and understood in terms of English ideological stereotypes. According to this vision, the paternal white civilizer rescued the blacks — slaves or descendants of slaves — and enabled them to accede to the universe of rational thought and the capitalist work ethic.

As far as the Hispanic world was concerned, a mythical version of historical events was elaborated, centered on the "black legend" of the Spanish conquest and colonization of the New World. In his essay "Power," included in *The Overcrowded Baracoon*, Naipaul warns against the false consciousness that has been generated in relation to the Hispanic and Hispanic-American world: "The blacks of British Honduras, in their one lazy, mosquito-infested town, reject 'Latinization' without knowing what they are rejecting.... The days of slavery were recalled with pride as the days when blacks and their English owners, friends really, stood shoulder to shoulder against the awful Spaniards. The blacks, at the end of the day, see themselves as British, made in the image of their former owners.... Latin Americans are seen as chaotic, violent, without the rule of law."[4]

However, it is obvious that imperial conflicts did not develop unilaterally. The two empires involved in the conquest and colonization of the Caribbean fought to maintain their hegemony with all the arms at their disposal — including the ideological and epistemological. The Guyanese writer Jan Carew suggested precisely that when, in his essay "Lever for Change: Cultural Identity in the Caribbean," he insisted that all the conquerors behaved in more or less the same way when it came to establishing their control.[5] So that, while the

English offered in their historical texts a detailed account of the genocide committed by Spain in America, the Spaniards, for their part, also highlighted the barbarities committed by the English and preferred to present their own achievements as the expression of a supposed Latin humanism. "The Anglo-Saxon colonization is populate and exploit; populate the new territories and exploit them adequately in terms of its own interests. By way of contrast, the Iberian conquest and colonization is incorporate and save; incorporate a new world into the Catholic empire and save souls for Christ.... It is a religious and missionary vision of the colonization process which is totally lacking in the Anglo-Saxon colonization."[6]

In his historical essay, *The Loss of El Dorado*, Naipaul attempts a revision of those constant strains in the historical accounts and attempts to present a synthesis of the contrasting ideological versions of the Spanish colonization. This attempt to demystify the received versions unfortunately does not overcome altogether existing ambivalences and, as a result, introduces mere reformulations of the stereotypes offered by Spanish and English historiography. For Naipaul, the Spanish colonization was chaotic and lacked serious objectives, given that those it professed were totally inadequate to the new reality. The image Naipaul offers of the Spanish conquerors and colonizers reflects his image of Latin America: lawless, bureaucratic, and indolent; their islands were lost because of negligence and a lack of clear objectives.

But, at the same time, he affirms that the Hispanic paradigm reflects an anti-utilitarian sense of life, which prefers honors to the accumulation of capital and thus transforms any unfortunate adventure into an heroic gesture, as in the case of the unsuccessful search for El Dorado.[7] Naipaul regards these characteristics as positive. Nevertheless, in general, when it is a question of analyzing the conquest and colonization of the New World, more or less anything that has been analyzed in positive terms in Spanish historiography is repudiated by the English and vice versa, so much so that villains are transformed into heroes depending on the version (the most spectacular case, Sir Francis Drake). According to Germán Arciniegas: "In the schools of the [Spanish-speaking] Caribbean, you will learn that in the sixteenth century, there was a bandit — Drake — whose pastimes included hanging friars and spitting on the Virgin's image; and horrified children make the sign of the Cross. But if they were to travel to London, they would be stupefied because one of the first things they would be shown is the table where Queen Elizabeth 'was honored to dine with Drake.' This is all very interesting because it indicates that history has two faces. Everything depends on the side of the fence from which you observe it."[8]

These historical considerations are very important for any study of mutual perceptions between Latin America and the English-speaking Caribbean because they illustrate the way in which each group came to form an image of the other as placed precisely on "the other side of the fence" and, in consequence, became out of touch with its own historically acquired values. It is also significant that, for a long time, the duality of the American continent, understood as the opposition between North America and South America or between English America and Spanish America, was seen from an Hispanic perspective in such a way that the values of English culture were reduced to those revealed by its hegemonic pretensions:

> Gentlemen of the marvelous and fertile North,
> the center is also part of the earthly globe.
> A wild audacity of nature's design
> made these poor Antilles a simple appendage of America.
> ...
> We understand the mysteries of Philosophy
> and Art inspired in sacred poetry.
> ...
> Excuse us, Gentlemen, if we do not understand
> your legal concepts of upright men.
> ...
> We do not understand, in these historical backwaters,
> the tongue or the feelings of the English peoples.
> We speak another language, with other thoughts
> tuned in to the spirit and the wind.[9]

The Spanish-speaking Caribbean countries will be surprised to find that these sentiments and the very language of the English peoples, repudiated for their identification with the values of subjection and domination, were also to be found in other countries belonging to the suffering center, to the "poor Antilles." Nevertheless, we need to appreciate that the identification of these values with the other pole of the North-South America duality matured during the course of the nineteenth century and a great part of the present century. It would be, therefore, unhistorical to expect that new values could be assumed from one day to another in response to the recent geopolitical order in the continent.

On the other hand, interpretations of the struggle for and the achievement of independence, in both groups of countries, have not been more fortunate than those we have already analyzed in relation to the conquest and colonization. Each group of countries regards its own process of independence as better, which means loaded historical accounts and a tendency to evaluate the actual sociocultural situation in terms of superiority/inferiority. For Naipaul, in *The Loss of El Dorado*, the Hispanic-American independence war loses its character as an heroic struggle for emancipation and is reduced to a farce, one more illusion in the dream world of the Latin American continent. In the same way, the intellectual author of the independent

Colombian state and of its constitution "... was a fraud. Miranda sought to convert himself into the Inca-Emperor of Hispanic America."[10] His dreams of independence did not include the blacks. He was a European dandy, accustomed to life in the court, the first cultured South American Europe had known, a decadent though sympathetic adventurer who offered to the Europeans the prefabricated image they wanted to receive of South America. In this book, the ideas of independence were a mere product of the delirious rhetoric of the South Americans — "for if it is a question of words, the Venezuelans have never been short of them"[11] — until the simulated blood was transformed into real blood that began to flow along the continental routes. In this way, the author sums up the central experience that gave birth to the Hispanic-American nationalities: Everything is a mask, a confusion of reality with the dreams of grandeur invented by a few Europeanized American "señoritos."

However, from the Hispanic-American point of view, there is an apparent conviction that an independence without bloodshed is hardly worthwhile, as it amounts to little more than a purely formal, juridical declaration of principles. This can be appreciated even in statements that adopt an objective tone, trying to explain differences without falling into the temptation of assuming valuative judgments: "The relatively pacific transition from colonial status to independence [in the English-speaking Caribbean countries]. . . produces a different level of consciousness if compared with that of countries like Cuba, where a hundred years of struggle were of fundamental importance in the forging of a strong national consciousness and a revolutionary ideology."[12]

In this affirmation, there is an apparent identification of the firmness of national consciousness with an experience of revolutionary struggle, from which one can deduce that peaceful independence is associated with a weak national consciousness. In the Hispanic-American tradition, as is evident, this is regarded as a negative characteristic of a nationality acquired without effort and calls into question the right to exercise political autonomy.

In both discourses, there is a central ingredient that has proved a formidable obstacle in the relations between Latin America and the English-speaking Caribbean: the notion of "race," which inevitably tugs historical accounts toward reductionist interpretations. If we return to Naipaul's text, there is a clear intention of relating the Hispanic-American independence wars to a specific racial ideal. In his portrait of Francisco Miranda, the Spanish revolutionary, the author says, "He knew how to exploit his attractive features: and the Hispanic American revolution was one of them.... Were there blacks in Hispanic America? No, or very few; the South Americans were Spaniards, or Amerindians, descendants of the Incas, a noble people anxious to achieve its freedom. The blacks were to be found in Trinidad and other Spanish islands in the West Indies but did not really belong to Colombia. Both Miranda and his colleagues would gladly surrender all these islands, with the exception of Cuba, in exchange for English support."[13]

In this sense, when the Liberators used the word "American," they referred only to certain of the ethnocultural groups, excluding the population of African origin. Thus, Naipaul repeats the criterion that the distance between Latin America and the English-speaking Caribbean was based on racial differences. According to this version, in Latin America, "criollo" society was made up of mestizos and white "criollos" who neglected the aspirations and necessities of the Afro-American population. In order to liberate their race, these Hispanic-American groups had handed over the "black islands" to the English slave owners. The implications of this interpretation of Latin American and Caribbean history are obvious.

Latin Americans contributed to a racial interpretation of these historical events when they accepted that their territory receive a denomination that amounted to taking part in the nineteenth-century discussion over the characterization of the four "great civilizing races." The only part of the globe that is identified by a name referring to its racial characteristics is Latin America; as a result, the ethnocultural complexity of the continent is summed up unilaterally in terms of the dominant group, which naturally emphasized the common European roots of the different nations.

Among Latin American authors, Nicolás Guillén preserved the possibilities of this cultural identification, despite the fact that his poetry was based on the search of what he himself defined as a "mestizo-black" aesthetic: "What belongs to us, which is much closer to the Latin spirit inherited from Spain, France and Portugal, that is what I feel is really mine, to be embraced close to my heart."[14]

On the other hand, in the English-speaking Caribbean, the gradual search for a cultural identity that would reflect the genuine characteristics of the majorities began to emerge and led many intellectuals to reevaluate the cultural links with African civilizations. The conception that oriented this process was "Afro-Antillean," and one of its fundamental pillars has been Edward K. Brathwaite, who recreated aesthetically Aimé Cesaire's odyssey — *The Notebooks on Returning to My Mother Country* — in the trilogy *The Arrivants.*[15] In the mental structures of the English-speaking Caribbean, the notion of "Afro-Antillean" as the most appropriate identification of what is Caribbean definitely took root. Thus, we can appreciate that when the English-speaking Caribbean relates to Latin America, on both sides there are racial elements incorporated into their respective ways of identifying themselves: the "Latin" and the "Afro-Antillean." As a result, it is hardly surprising that the initial contacts between the two groups of countries were plagued by prejudices and mistrust.

Nevertheless, the Latin American Caribbean countries, basically the Spanish-speaking islands and Haiti, have now incorporated "Caribbeanism" as a dimension of their culture and, to that extent, have contributed to bridging the gap between the two realities. The notion of "Afro-Antillean" is the key element that draws them together and calls for a revision of the racial conceptions traditionally accepted in the Latin American continent. In this sense, one can consider the Cubans Nicolás Guillén and Regino Pedroso, together with the Haitian Jacques Stephen Alexis, genuine spokesmen of the idea of the "Caribbean" as the essential point of reference for cultures and peoples, applicable wherever genuine cultural experiences are reproduced.[16]

Perceived Reality:
The Image of the "Other" in Terms of Values

The traditional relation between the two groups was marked by an evident influence of stereotypes and by the insignificant or nonexistent attention paid to the "other" in the elaboration of their respective identities. As a result, neither West Indians nor Latin Americans appear as genuine protagonists in the literature of the other group. What can be found are mere shadows that drift along the pages anxious to come to terms with a reality to which they clearly belong but which is alien to them: In a Cuban setting, "Maud is the splendid Jamaican woman, with her snow-white tunic, who looks after the house. The owners never visit. But the existence of Maud is only to be captured by checking the windows, with their impeccable lace curtains, permanently closed in order to keep out the dust."[17]

In the English-speaking Caribbean, we can also find references of this type. In *The Jubillous Mountains*, by Roger Mais, "the Cuban" is an accessory character — whose identification by his nationality says more than a proper name — a prisoner who, together with Surgue, the central character, attempts to escape from prison.[18] The places reserved for "the others" are, therefore, depressing: prisons, the stifling heat and agony of the sugar plants, behind the curtains of a rich house. There is no space for a vital expressiveness in a literature that relegates them to the shadows. There are, however, occasional descriptive references to these shadows, which serve to judge, by extension, the culture to which they belong. Thus, for example, we can read in Naipaul's tale *The Middle Passage* that a group of travelers, from the English-speaking Caribbean and tourists, who are crossing the ocean from Europe to Trinidad, complain about the conditions of the ship, the food, and the lack of cleanliness; the author considers that this is due to the fact that it is a Spanish ship.[19]

Nevertheless, in occasional texts that explore the existence of the other more closely, these shadows are converted into The Shadow, that is to say, into the cultural complex that limits the growth of the psyche: The Shadow is the alien spirit that invades and occupies one's physical, moral, or spiritual vital living space; or, expressed in other terms, "it is that which we ignore about ourselves."[20] In the novel *Ecué-Yamba-O*, Alejo Carpentier captures this sentiment of Cuban workers displaced by Jamaicans in the sugar plant: "Menegildo crossed several crowded alleys.... He felt strange among so many blacks with other customs and a different language. The Jamaicans were a bunch of presumptuous bastards and animals! The Haitians were animals, savages! ... What good had been the War of Independence, which political orators so loved to recall, if one was to be continually displaced by these bastards?..."[21]

In the tale, Menegildo accuses these "foreigners" of abuses and murders, even when he is conscious that their participation has been no more than indirect. The psyche has to defend itself from the intrusion of the shadow — or, to repeat, of the unknown — elaborating fantasies that serve to affirm its own superiority: "... the job of a cart driver still has some advantages.... The pressure of the siren is more or less bearable and from the height of the driving seat, you can look down on the Jamaicans with their felt hats, who are frankly despicable, even though they proudly declare themselves 'citizens of the United Kingdom of Great Britain.'"[22]

The intention of the author of this text is not to express his own perception of the "others" portrayed in this context but, rather, most Cuban workers' perceptions of Jamaicans in the sugar plants. The evaluation of the other collectivity in terms of superiority/inferiority is a constant in the contacts between the two groups. Naipaul also understands this, commenting that the English-speaking Caribbean, like many of the English themselves, despise everything Spanish. An indication of this is that "West Indians are English-speaking and when confronted with the foreigner display the language arrogance of all English-speaking people."[23] In all these cases, the prevailing ignorance means that any approximation to the reality of "the others" is charged with valuative connotations that automatically exclude the possibility of establishing relations on grounds of equality.

Furthermore, anyone who examines a new reality from outside, without any real attempt to inform himself about it, tends to see it as chaotic. This can be seen in *Vision of Guyana* by the Cuban writer Joaquín Santana: "Guyana is complex, interesting, mysterious, surprising. No. That's not enough. One doesn't know how to describe such an incongruent disorder of races, religions, and customs, all existing together in a single place, under the same flag."[24]

It is also significant that in an attempt to find points of contact between the reality that he is observing and what he actually sees, a geographical image supposedly decisive for any definition of the Caribbean leads to a distorted perception. This is the case when the author describes the waters that wash the Guyanese coast: "Here the Caribbean — and it's a fact worth stressing —

loses its intense, transparent, beautiful blue color and the sea becomes dark, dense, disagreeable. It is not even pleasant to observe. It provokes a disagreeable sensation even stronger than the beautiful image of this sea registered in the memory."[25]

It is evident that in making this comparison, the author ignores the fact that the water on the Guyanese coast does not form part of the Caribbean Sea, but of the ocean which, furthermore, receives the impact of the enormous rivers whose deltas punctuate the coast between the Orinoco and the Amazon rivers. The result is a deformed characterization of both Guyana and the Caribbean and an inevitable failure to understand the imagery that relates the Guyanese to his surroundings.

Of course, not all evaluations are of this nature. Some, on the contrary, attempt to portray the reality of the "other" in positive terms, graciously recognizing the existence of "values," which turn out to be precisely those characteristics on the basis of which the Europeans measure the universality of a determined culture. The idea of Latin America — together with the Caribbean — as the continent of the "real-marvelous," although it was formulated with the intention of recuperating the visions of the world of its different communities, was nonetheless oriented by a search for legitimacy in the eyes of the Europeans and stimulated by the hope that "the world" would recognize its aesthetic propositions as valid. Together with the phrase: "Here the Exquisite Corpse strolls along the streets,"[26] which Carpentier puts into the mouth of one of his characters, as a gift clearly offered to the European surrealists, the description of the marvels always is based on classical elements drawn from European culture: "Amongst the extraordinary diversity there is apparently a common denominator ... music. To the Caribbean islands one could well have applied the name which Rabelais, the great classic [writer] of the French Renaissance, gave to some islands which he called 'lands to be listened to.'"[27]

On the basis of this conception, for example, the author comments that the island of Barbados possesses an "immense culture," given that, apart from its excellent prose writers and good newspapers, the radio offers generous coverage of classical music, and Handel's "Hallelujah" identifies one of the stations, "in the same way as in Trinidad, where Bach is interpreted by the steel bands."[28]

Nevertheless, while the approximation is always critical, in these works one can also find the desire for closer links, based on a common geographical destiny — the historically conditioned isolation, the sea as a bridge and a barrier, the eternal hurricanes — and certain affinities between their cultural experiences: "But now one-footed Osaín, lord of the cyclones, genius of rotation, of gyrating dances, had taken to dancing from the mouth of the Mississippi to the Orinoco Delta, and dancing rumbas, congas, sons, calypsos, contradanzas...."[29]

Broader Reality:
The Image of the Other in Terms of Relations

C loser contacts between the two groups were encouraged, in the case of some Caribbean and Latin American writers, by the very geographical contiguity. This prompted the conviction, at an intuitive level, that there had to be similarities, despite the stereotypes and the dissimilar colonial legacies. In most cases, the possibility of sharing and incorporating the experiences of the others is expressed with evident emotion. This is the case of the series of poems, written in 1934, which Nicolás Guillén published as *West Indies LTD*, three decades before contacts began at an official level. In these texts, apart from the emotive perceptions, one can capture cognitive necessities and excruciating efforts to portray the real anxieties of the Antillean peoples:

> West Indies! West Indies! West Indies!
> This is a hard-skinned people,
> copper-colored, many-headed and life belly-crawling
> with dry mud encrusted to the skin.
> ...
> This is the people who are "all right"
> when everything is real bad;
> this is the people who are "very well"
> when nobody is well at all.[30]

For some authors, the racial characterization of the region, instead of constituting an obstacle, serves as a bridge between the English-speaking Caribbean countries and those that are Spanish-speaking. In this sense, the poetry of Regino Pedroso deserves a mention. Others, however, like Naipaul, regard the search for similarities on the basis of racial criteria as evidence of a false consciousness that would limit the development of the societies which make up the West Indies. One needs to appreciate that Naipaul, a Trinidadian of Hindu descent, could hardly identify himself with a conception of the Caribbean constructed on the basis of images of Africanism. For him, the contacts need to go beyond mere formalities, because the English-speaking Caribbean — "For nothing was created in the British West Indies, no civilization as in Spanish America...." — by incorporating itself into Latin America, would gain not only a continent but also a civilization.[31] However, the idea of the Afro-Antillean as the essence of the Caribbean soul impedes the perception of this possibility: "In the islands, in fact, black identity is a sentimental trap, obscuring the issues. What is needed is access to a society, larger in every sense, where people will be allowed to grow. For some territories, this larger society may be Latin American."[32]

Naipaul's opinion, in this case and in others that reflect similar perceptions, has always provoked a bitter reaction on the part of some sectors of Caribbean intellectuals, who are unwilling to accept Latin America as a point of reference. In general, the most that has been acceptable in the English-speaking Caribbean is the possibility of tightening links with some of the Spanish-speaking Caribbean countries, especially the islands, with which they share certain socioeconomic and cultural characteristics.

Beginning in the 1960s, when the road to decolonization was being discussed in the area, several Latin American countries began to "discover" their Caribbean features and reclaim their place along with the West Indies, and various Latin American states assumed the need to tighten links as a strategy. In this context, the initiatives of the Cuban state stand out, reflected in different types of official activity. In 1972, diplomatic relations were established with Guyana, Trinidad and Tobago, Jamaica, and Barbados, accompanied by expressions of a profound identification with the Caribbean spirit. In the field of literature, it was significant that, in 1976, the basis of the *Casa de las Américas* prizes was broadened in order to include the literature of the West Indies while, at the same time, translations were published of the works of major authors: Edward K. Brathwaite, Angus Richmond, George Lamming, Roger Mais, and James Carnegie figure among the personalities that *Casa de las Américas* has begun to divulge in the Spanish-speaking world. In this way, Cuba acquired a clear leadership in Caribbean cultural activity, to such a point that Victor Stafford Reid could refer on one occasion, and in Spanish, to "nuestra casa caribeña."[33]

To the extent that these links have become institutionalized, a literature has also emerged, basically in Cuba, which is more pamphletary, basically responding to official policy but without an adequate exploration of the aesthetic dimension of its imagery. An example is the poem *The Islands and the Fireflies*, written by the Cuban Cos Causse and describing the West Indies in a prefabricated language, with Cuba at its side as a source of inspiration:

Trinidad and Tobago, separated by sirens and dreams,
and by the Phillips Petroleum Company and the Standard
    Oil Co., among others:
but sometimes she refuses to receive blows and reacts
    with hate against the homicide.
Barbados, which is all at sea, and cannot reach the port
and inclines herself to entertain tourists and foreign
    prostitutes:
but curses in the tongue of the indian assassinated
    during the discovery.
Dominica, so small, such a little girl and
    violated so often:
but now grown stronger and waiting for the return
    of the pirates.
And others who I do not name now because they were
    even robbed of their palm trees.

And Cuba is full of a fire which burns vigorously
and offers it to them.[34]

'   Apparently, the central objective of this type of poetry, independent of any analysis of its literary merits, is to show the English-speaking world that Cuban society takes it into account, in both its literature and its struggles. It hardly needs to be said that, in these cases, the search for closer relations neither presupposes comprehension nor does it contribute to it.

On the other hand, this same dynamic is also present when personalities in literary texts formulate declarations of principle related to the theme. Thus, a personality in the novel *A Kind of Living*, written by the Guyanese Angus Richmond, says, "I, at least, am opposed to the idea of returning to Africa.... We should establish new roots here in Guyana. There shouldn't be conflicts between the races. There is room for all of us here. Develop the resources we possess, learn to live together, establishing contacts with our neighbors in the Caribbean and in South America. What a grand prospect!"[35]

Expressed in this way, none of the multiple forms that closer ties between the two regions could assume of itself presupposes a prior comprehension of the reality of the other. The two previous examples indicate no more than that there is a consciousness of the existence of the other and that, as a result, it seems logical that there should be contact. Nevertheless, the manifestation of a willingness to assume a determined attitude by no means implies a necessary modification in valuative perceptions, even though it is true that the establishment of links, whether spontaneous or official, can contribute to a comprehension of the other and, as a result, to a symbolic appropriation of his reality.

Appropriated Reality:
The Image of the Other at the Level of Comprehension

In order to comprehend the other, one needs to accept that differences do not mean inequalities and that, in consequence, the cultural symbols of a different reality are as valid as one's own in terms of their role in the recreation and interpretation of reality. Some approximations to this type of cognitive appropriation can be discerned in the field of literature. One of the first steps in this direction was undoubtedly taken by Nicolás Guillén who, in all his writings, sustained the thesis that the ethnocultural differences between the Spanish-speaking Antilles and the West Indies could not be used to disguise the fact that the two regions suffered the same situation of dependence. It is precisely on the basis of this conviction that he proposed his definition of "mestizo-blackness" for the Hispanic Caribbean, as against the idea of *negritude*, which authors from the French-speaking Caribbean were proposing in the 1930s:

I greet you, Tropic.
Greeting of a sportsman,
spring-like,
which escapes from my salted lung
across these islands, scandalously sons of yours.
(Jamaica says
that she is content to be black,
and Cuba is already aware that she is mulatta.)[36]

In the West Indian context, the condition of "mulatto," apart from the negative connotations for the black majorities, is associated explicitly with the elites who sought to transform themselves into the leaders of their countries, a connotation clearly different from that which it has in the Spanish-speaking countries. For this reason, Guillén's use of the expression, understood beyond its function in the poetic act, is an attempt to establish differences on the basis of equality.

To the extent that this dynamic has been developed, various authors have managed to imagine an essential unity of the Antillean world without referring to a definition of the basic elements of such an identity. In his poem *Calypso*, which is a call for the auto-affirmation of the insular Caribbean, Edward K. Brathwaite reveals this consciousness of unity from the very first lines:

The stones have slipped along a curve and
    flowered as islands:
Cuba and Santo Domingo
Jamaica and Puerto Rico
Grenada Guadeloupe Bonaire
Curved stone which whistles toward the cliffs
Waves teethed in pottery
White foam which splinters in atoms
Betsabé Montego Bay shorelines
Arching flowering in the summer.[37]

A similar consciousness is expressed, in a different type of discourse, by Manuel Zapata Olivella in his *Changó, el gran putas*, offering a new version of the historical processes that led to the emergence of the American sociopolitical and cultural formations, attributing the most important roles to the descendants of Africans. The main thread of the history is in the hands of *ovishas* and American gods — no longer archetypes provided by the Greco-Roman pantheon as a symbolic offering of "Western civilization" — who lead their peoples toward the final liberation of humanity: "Our religion will grow in America and in the entire world, and you are not capable of preventing our Ancestors, African and American, from uniting us, strengthening us and teaching us how to struggle for the liberation of Humanity from the insanity of the White Wolf. Changó has spoken!"[38]

It can also be observed that gradually the conviction is growing that the different cultural formations, both in the English-speaking Caribbean and in continental Latin America, are equally products of colonial exploitation and that the essential similarity of these processes needs to be recognized. Furthermore, for the English-speaking Caribbean, this perception offers the possibility of appropriating the continental referent:

> For four hundred years
>   Out of Ngola
> forty people
>   Turned up on the plantations of Brazil
> every week very weak
> or in the plantations of the sea
> dead
>   Every Sunday
> as I sugar my tea
> I want to shoot somebody.[39]

Within this ideological perspective, Cuba becomes a symbol accessible to various sectors of the West Indian intellectuals, who adopt the Cuban Revolution as a "model." One tendency that can be observed in a certain type of poetry in the English-speaking Caribbean has an explicit sociopolitical content, inspired in the struggle of the nations for their dignity, in an anti-imperialism that represents a confrontation with the colonial values of the European metropolis and the neocolonialism of the United States. In this sense, Cuba served as a nearby example of the realization of a collective aspiration: to escape from the structural inequalities of Latin America and the Caribbean. On the other hand, the incorporation of these nations into the Movement of Non-Aligned Countries, where Cuba exercised an effective leadership, conditioned the nature of this symbolic appropriation. George Lamming comments on this situation: "As far as priorities are concerned, the political struggle stands out as the most urgent of our tasks. And now we have a heroic example with the miraculous birth and flowering of the Cuban Revolution. The struggle was protagonized by the Cuban people, but the victory was not exclusively for the Cubans; it should be acknowledged eternally with an embrace which covers the entire Caribbean, and defended where necessary with the pride and firmness of the entire Caribbean."[40]

As Jan Carew sees it, the example of Cuba and its revolution constitutes a synthesis of the eternal struggle in America, of different nations and colors, against their subjection and exploitation. A synthesis of this type is obliged to resort to images somewhat out of context in order to legitimize itself: "It ... was as if Zam Zam had been reborn from the ashes of the Palmares Republic; as if Boni was encouraging them from his woods in Suriname, and together with all this were the voices of Caonabo, Anacaona, Paramaconi ... and millions of anonymous figures who proclaim their solidarity across the centuries."[41]

Nevertheless, this type of cognitive approximation to the social processes of a Latin American country is not devoid of valuative judgments, among which those related to racial problems acquire a significant weight. How were the Antillean blacks to appropriate symbolically a revolutionary process whose leaders were in their majority white? Valuative judgments intervene in order to adapt the symbol to established criteria for interpreting reality; in this sense, the same author puts the following comment into the mouth of an old Guyanese man on the occasion of Fidel's visit to his country: "But look how they lie to us. They told us that Fidel Castro was white. This man is not white, because he does not behave like a white man."[42]

This example clearly indicates that knowledge does not always contribute to a transformation of valuative schemes and that, in many cases, it is the evaluations that determine cognitive necessities.

In practice, this was the imagery that allowed Grenada to open itself to the Latin American conception of social revolution, transforming the traditional West Indian perception of Latin American violence and political chaos into a noble struggle for social equality and justice. Thus, Grenada could be registered in the annals of Latin American "liberating heroism":

Nicaragua-Grenada,
Carnivals of Liberty,
converge
in the Plaza de la Revolution
and in Carenage,
the tongues of the Bells of Liberty
toll across our Caribbean....[43]

On this point what remains to be said is that although the Cuban model no longer retains the same vigorous presence in the current propositions of West Indian literature, Cuba, nevertheless, continues to be a fundamental point of reference for the Caribbean in its actual imagery.

For our analysis, Guyana is another interesting case. In the Caribbean, according to whichever of the definitions is adopted, Guyana was an integral part of the historical formation of the West Indies and was almost totally isolated from the countries of the South American continent. Nevertheless, its inhabitants feel the need to share a common destiny with the continent. This feeling is present in the narratives and poetry of Wilson Harris. It is not that Harris refers to Latin America as a geopolitical category nor that he presents images of Latin America as references external to his own symbolic systems. In fact, Harris does not mention Latin America precisely because he expresses himself as an integral part of the continent, and symbolic references that are equally valid for Venezuelans, Brazilians, or Peruvians are vitally integrated into his imagery. It is significant that Harris had the advantage of living with the Amerindian population that inhabits the banks of the Essequibo and Delaware rivers, an experience which is not available in the insular Caribbean territories because of the literally devastating impact of European colonization on the indigenous population of the islands. In all his works, the author manages — by means of a dense, baroque imagery — to unite different cosmologies and produce a mixture of their respective symbolisms: as, for example, in the reconstruction of Caribbean myths realized in *The Sleepers of Roraima: A Carib Trilogy*.[44] In this sense, Harris, together with other Guyanese authors, such as Jan Carew, have contributed to Caribbean literature precisely its continental dimension.

In the perception of these authors, Latin America and the Caribbean are similar to the extent that both regions follow the subtle and unpredictable paths of miscegenation: "When I speak of the West Indies I am thinking of overlapping contexts of Central and South America as well.... The point I want to make in regard to the West Indies is that the pursuit of a strange and subtle goal — melting-pot, miscegenation, call it what you like — is the mainstream (though unacknowledged) tradition in the Americas."[45]

In his novels, Harris concentrates on producing alchemic combinations of different ethnocultural ingredients and of their corresponding symbols, with a view to achieving a cultural expression that reflects the originality and richness of American reality. Thus, for example, in his novel *Palace of the Peacock*, one of the key personalities is a mestizo called Schomburgh, the great-grandson of a German who had explored the continent during the nineteenth century and an Araucan Amerindian woman.[46] One of the characteristics of Harris's work is precisely the systematic exploration of the possibilities offered by experiences of miscegenation.

Jan Carew can be placed in this same perspective, although his work is directed more toward understanding and recuperating the original indigenous cultures and to reevaluating their symbolic systems. He is the author of several legend-tales whose central figure is one or another of the well-known personalities of the Amerindian cosmology, such as Amalivaca, a mythical hero present in the entire Caribbean. Carew, for the importance that he attributes to indigenous cultural elements in the formation of the Caribbean soul, expresses a vision open to Latin America: "The Caribbean writer and artist ... are compelled by history to move from one side to another, from the nucleus ... of cultural survivals to any of the regions of the twentieth century, the island, the continent or the cosmos, which his imagination can embrace; and to wander across the epochs of this continent stained with blood, in order to penetrate into the fathomless silences where the Amerindian past is buried...."[47]

This means that for Carew, the nutritional source of cultural symbols is to be found in indigenous cultural elements that are hidden behind the silence in the most diverse situations of the Latin American continent, and he proposes the assumption of these cultural contents in order to open up the possibilities of enrichment and firmer roots for the Caribbean soul. If the Caribbean intellectual has been defined continually as a nomad, the explanation is that he has lacked the land where his culture could be sown, for the limited space at his disposal has always belonged to foreigners. In the words of the author, the way to remedy this situation is by assuming the memory of the Caribs, "the Human Beings, the Vagabonds of Dreaming Time."[48]

In synthesis, there is an image of Latin America as a continent with regenerating symbols that need to be explored by the inhabitants of the English-speaking Caribbean, not only in its search for roots but also as valid references in the creation of a meaning for life in the West Indies. It also offers a way of resolving the traditional dual reference that presented cultural options in terms of two distant continents, Europe and Africa. To this extent, comprehension implies a transformation of values and access to the elaboration of perceptions other than the traditional, in the case of those countries that make up the two regions, Latin America and the Caribbean.

Conclusions

Mutual perceptions between Latin America and the Caribbean are nowadays still in an embryonic state, if we are to judge on the basis of the literary production of the two groups of countries. In these, images have been established that account for the existence of "the other"; however, what has predominated is a condemnatory posture rather than an attempt to increase comprehension. But this situation tends to change to the extent that — within a new geopolitical situation — contacts are consolidated that have a clear resonance in collective emotions and attitudes, as we have been able to appreciate in our review of the works produced since the 1960s.

It is safe to say that these preliminary indications in the field of literature are a clear reflection of the state of mutual perceptions in other areas. As an example of this, the reference that Cuba has become a "model" of social revolution for the English-speaking Caribbean not only has been reflected in this literature; it was clearly manifested in the political practice of a particular country during the Grenadian revolution. What needs to be asked is whether this was a mere, isolated incident or whether Latin America possesses symbolic values capable of being assumed as cultural referents by the West Indies in general.

According to what we saw in relation to Guyanese literature, the answer to this question is perhaps to be found in the immense possibilities that miscegenation offers — as the principal current that attracts all other cultural expressions in the American continent — and, in contrast, the world view of the Amerindian civilizations. Perhaps these two paths open access to the continent for the English-speaking Caribbean and present the region with the possibility of feeling a part of the wider American experience.

Notes

1. Tzvetan Todorov, 1987, *La conquista de América. La cuestión del otro* (Mexico: Siglo XXI Editores).

2. V.S. Naipaul, 1984, *Finding the Center (Two Narratives)* (New York: Alfred A. Knopf), 35.

3. Ian Munro and Reinhard Sander, 1972, "Interview with George Lamming," in *Kas-Kas* (Austin: African and Afro-American Research Institute, University of Texas), 18.

4. V.S. Naipaul, 1984, "Power," in *The Overcrowded Barracoon and Other Articles* (New York: Penguin Books), 275.

5. Jan Carew, 1980, "Palancas para el cambio. Identidad cultural en el Caribe," *Casa de las Américas*, (Havana) 118 (January-February): 61-69.

6. José Luis Abellán, 1972, *La idea de América* (Madrid: Ediciones Istmo), 45.

7. See V.S. Naipaul, 1970, *The Loss of El Dorado* (Caracas: Monte Avila).

8. Germán Arciniegas, 1973, *Biografía del Caribe* (Buenos Aires: Editorial Sudamericana), 158.

9. José de Diego, "Aleluya. A los Caballeros del Norte," *Tricontinental,* (Havana), 43: 43-47.

10. Naipul 1970, 346.

11. Naipaul 1970, 359.

12. Blanca Acosta, Samuel Goldberg, and Ileana Sáenz, 1974, "Introducción a la narrativa antillana de lengua inglesa," *Casa de las Américas*, (Havana), 86(September-October): 37.

13. Naipaul 1970, 355.

14. Nicolás Guillén, 1975, *Prosa de prisa*, Vol. 1 (Havana: Editorial Arte y Literatura), 344.

15. The trilogy is made up of three volumes of poetry considered classics of West Indies literature: "Rights of Passage" (1967), "Masks" (1968), and "Islands" (1969). On this, see *The Arrivants*, 1973, (London: Oxford University Press).

16. The authors mentioned sustained this point of view during the entire course of their literary careers, and it is to be found in each and every one of their publications. Nevertheless, in some, the idea of the Caribbean as a harmonically achieved unity is more clearly expressed. For Guillén, see *West Indies LTD.* (1934) and *El Son Entero* (1943); for Pedroso, *Los días tumultuosos (1934-1936)*; and for Alexis, *L'Espace d'un Cillement*, n.d.

17. Elisio Diego, 1972, "La Penumbra," in *Nombrar las cosas* (Havana: Editorial UNEAC), 189.

18. Roger Mais, 1978, *Las montañas jubilosas* (Havana: Editorial Casa de las Américas).

19. V.S. Naipaul, [1962] 1981, *The Middle Passage* (New York: Vintage Books), 12-39.

20. Rafael López-Pedraza, 1987, *Ansiedad cultural* (Caracas: Editorial Psicología Arquetipal), 49.

21. Alejo Carpentier, 1977, *Ecué-Yamba-O* (Buenos Aires: Editorial Octavo Sello), 52.

22. Carpentier 1977, 24.

23. Naipaul 1981, 16.

24. Joaquín Santana, 1973, "Visión de Guyana," *Casa de las Américas*, (Havana), 78(May-June): 110-120 and 111.

25. Santana 1973, 120.

26. Alejo Carpentier, 1978, *La consagración de la primavera* (Mexico: Siglo XXI Editores), 337.

27. Alejo Carpentier, 1980, "La cultura de los pueblos que habitan en las tierras del Mar Caribe," *Casa de las Américas*, (Havana), 118(January-February), 3.

28. Carpentier 1980, 2.

29. Carpentier 1978, 86.

30. Nicolás Guillén, 1972, *Obra poética*, Vol. 1, (Havana: Instituto Cubano del Libro), 166.

31. Naipaul 1981, 27.

32. Naipaul 1984, 274.

33. Victor Stafford Reid, 1980, "Identidad cultural en el Caribe," *Casa de las Américas*, (Havana), 118(January-February): 48.

34. Cos Causse, 1978, "Las islas y las luciérnagas," *Casa de las Américas*, (Havana), 108(May-June): 51-55.

35. Angus Richmond, *A Kind of Living,* 32, quoted by Lisa Davis, 1981, "La Casa de las Américas y la literatura antillana de lengua inglesa," *Casa de las Américas*, (Havana), 128(September-October): 112.

36. Guillén 1972, 136.

37. Edward K. Brathwaite, 1980, "Calypso," *Casa de las Américas*, (Havana), 221(July-August): 100.

38. Manuel Zapata Olivella, 1984, *Changó, el gran putas* (Bogotá: Editorial Oveja Negra), 361.

39. Shake Kean, poem reproduced in *One a Week with Water. Rhymes and Notes*, quoted in Davis 1981, 109.

40. George Lamming, 1980, "Identidad cultural en el Caribe insular," *Casa de las Américas*, (Havana), 118(January-February): 27.

41. Jan Carew, 1979a, "Lo que la Revolución Cubana significa para mí," *Casa de las Américas*, (Havana), 112(January-February): 22.

42. Carew 1979a, 25.

43. Jan Carew, 1979b, "Nicaragua-Grenada. De una crisálida de arco iris," *Casa de las Américas*, (Havana), 117(November-December): 120.

44. Wilson Harris, 1970, *The Sleepers of Roraima: A Carib Trilogy* (London: Faber).

45. Wilson Harris, 1967, *Tradition, the Writer and Society* (London and Port of Spain: New Beacon Publications), 31-32.

46. Wilson Harris, 1960, *Palace of the Peacock* (London: Faber).

47. Jan Carew, 1978, "El escritor caribeño y el exilio," *Casa de las Américas*, (Havana), 105(November-December): 49.

48. Jan Carew, 1983, "Credo Caribe," *Casa de las Américas*, (Havana), 139(July-August) and in Carew 1987, (Port of Spain: New Beacon Publications), 68-88.

References

Abellán, José Luis. 1972. *La idea de América*. Madrid: Ediciones Istmo.

Acosta, Blanca, Samuel Goldberg, and Ileana Sáenz. 1974. "Introducción a la narrativa antillana de lengua inglesa." *Casa de las Américas* (Havana) 86 (September-October).

Alexis, Jacques Stephen. N.d. *L'Espace d'un Cillement*.

Arciniegas, Germán. 1973. *Biografía del Caribe*. Buenos Aires: Editorial Sudamericana.

Brathwaite, Edward K. 1973. *The Arrivants*. London: Oxford University Press.

Brathwaite, Edward K. 1980. "Calypso." *Casa de las Américas* (Havana) 221 (July-August).

Carew, Jan. 1978. "El escritor caribeño y el exilio." *Casa de las Américas* (Havana) 105 (November-December).

Carew, Jan. 1979a. "Lo que la Revolución Cubana significa para mí." *Casa de las Américas* (Havana) 112 (January-February).

Carew, Jan. 1979b. "Nicaragua-Grenada. De una crisálida de arco iris." *Casa de las Américas* (Havana) 117 (November-December).

Carew, Jan. 1980. "Palancas para el cambio. Identidad cultural en el Caribe." *Casa de las Américas* (Havana) 118 (January-February).

Carew, Jan. 1983. "Credo Caribe." *Casa de las Américas* (Havana) 139 (July-August).

Carpentier, Alejo. 1977. *Ecué-Yamba-O*. Buenos Aires: Editorial Octavo Sello.

Carpentier, Alejo. 1978. *La consagración de la primavera*. Mexico: Siglo XXI Editores.

Carpentier, Alejo. 1980. "La cultura de los pueblos que habitan en las tierras de Mar Caribe." *Casa de las Américas* (Havana) 118 (January-February).

Causse, Cos. 1978. "Las islas y las luciérnagas." *Casa de las Américas* (Havana) 108 (May-June).

Davis, Lisa. 1981. "La Casa de las Américas y la literatura antillana de lengua inglesa." *Casa de las Américas* (Havana) 128 (September-October).

de Diego, José. "Aleluya. A los Caballeros del Norte." *Tricontinental* (Havana)43.

Diego, Elisio. 1972. "La Penumbra." In *Nombrar las cosas*. Havana: Editorial UNEAC.

Guillén, Nicolás. 1934. *West Indies LTD*.

Guillén, Nicolás. 1943. *El Son Entero*.

Guillén, Nicolás. 1972. *Obra poética*, Vol. 1. Havana: Instituto Cubano del Libro.

Guillén, Nicolás. 1975. *Prosa de prisa,* Vol. 1. Havana: Editorial Arte y Literatura.

Harris, Wilson. 1960. *Palace of the Peacock*. London: Faber.

Harris, Wilson. 1967. *Tradition, the Writer and Society*. London, Port of Spain: New Beacon Publications.

Harris, Wilson. 1970. *The Sleepers of Roraima: A Carib Trilogy*. London: Faber.

Lamming, George. 1980. "Identidad cultural en el Caribe insular." *Casa de las Américas* (Havana) 118 (January-February).

López-Pedraza, Rafael. 1987. *Ansiedad cultural*. Caracas: Editorial Psicología Arquetipal.

Mais, Roger. 1978. *Las montañas jubilosas*. Havana: Editorial Casa de las Américas.

Munro, Ian, and Reinhard Sander. 1972. "Interview with George Lamming." In *Kas-Kas*, African and Afro-American Research Institute. Austin: University of Texas.

Naipaul, V.S. [1969] 1970. *The Loss of El Dorado*. Caracas: Monte Avila.

Naipaul, V.S. [1962] 1981. *The Middle Passage*. New York: Vintage Books.

Naipaul, V.S. 1984a. "Power." In *The Overcrowded Barracoon and Other Articles*. New York: Penguin Books.

Naipaul, V.S. 1984b. *Finding the Center (Two Narratives)*. New York: Alfred A. Knopf.

Pedroso, Regino. N.d. *Los días tumultuosos (1934-1936)*.

Santana, Joaquín. 1973. "Visión de Guyana." *Casa de las Américas* (Havana) 78(May-June).

Stafford Reid, Victor. 1980. "Identidad cultural en el Caribe." *Casa de las Américas* (Havana) 118 (January-February).

Todorov, Tzvetan. 1987. *La conquista de América. La cuestión del otro*. Mexico: Siglo XXI Editores.

Zapata Olivella, Manuel. 1984. *Changó, el gran putas*. Bogota: Editorial Oveja Negra.

Chapter Five

The Caribbean and Hemispheric Cooperation: A Multilateral Perspective

Christopher R. Thomas

The twentieth century can be described as a period of profound upheavals in the history of humanity. The fall of the Austro-Hungarian Empire, coupled with its consequences for the political, military, and sociological configuration in Europe, introduced a twentieth century that will go down in history as the era when the world came of age through successive periods of violent open conflict, Cold War hostilities, politico-economic transformations, and technological landmarks, all of which have shaped the destiny of humanity as never before.

The First World War, the Russian Revolution, and World War II with its aftermath revolutionalized the world from many perspectives; particular examples are the creation of new independent states in Europe, the division of the political and economic world, and the further consolidation of this division through the decolonization process. Simultaneous with the Cold War hostilities that marked the 1950s, 1960s, and 1970s was the birth and development of a technological and technologically motivated industrial revolution, mainly in the West. While it influenced in many respects the political and military hostilities in the first instance, the technological revolution itself very rapidly superseded them in dynamism, relevance, and importance. It was not surprising, therefore, that by the 1980s, the stage was set for the introduction of a new era in human development in which there are important new constituent elements — namely, technology, economics, trade, the environment, and the dawn of a new and more complex social environment.

Though the Iron Curtain of the political, military, and economic divide was centered figuratively in Europe, it literally demarcated two poles of conflicting ideologies, one centered in the East and the other in the West. The Western Hemisphere became center stage in the conflict, providing a new dimension to inter-hemispheric relations and priorities precisely at the time when these were being explored in the development of the Pan-American Movement.

Since its beginning in 1889, notwithstanding the purely Latin American origin of the idea, the Pan-American Movement sought to express the political, cultural, economic, and social solidarity of member states of the Americas. In 1948, the formation of the Organization of American States (OAS) institutionalized Pan-Americanism and set the stage for deeper, broader, and more systematic cooperation among American states for the furtherance of peace and democracy in the hemisphere. In spite of its significance to European politics and economics in the previous centuries, the Caribbean as a political, economic, and social entity did not figure among the actors of the Pan-American agenda for quite some time. It was not until the introduction of the era of decolonization by the United Nations, after World War II, that more attention began to be paid to the "American" identity of the Caribbean Basin countries, both from outside and within the Caribbean region itself.

Geography, Politics, and History in Caribbean Hemispheric Cooperation

The geographical unity of the Caribbean, except for a brief period in the early days of Spanish colonization, never has represented a unified geopolitical factor in the hemispheric context. However, in spite of its disintegration into various subregional political groupings and its rigid casting in that mold (until the recent formation of the Association of Caribbean States — ACS), the geographical Caribbean represents a sizable, unique, varied, and strategic part of the Americas. Definitions of the Caribbean region vary. Developments over the last four years, however, have inevitably led to an admixture of considerations in the definition of the region, ranging from the historic to the sociocultural and political. More recent developmental evolution now permits a description, rather than a definition, of the region that encompasses all those islands and countries washed by the Caribbean Sea, plus Suriname, Guyana, The Bahamas, French Guiana (part of the historical Caribbean), as well as El Salvador, which, while not having a Caribbean coastline, is an integral part of Central America. This description may not be finite. The historic enigma of the region holds the continuing potential for further sociopolitical engagement. The vast kaleidoscope of mainland, coastlands, islands, sea, mountains, plains, climatic differences, and topographic variations makes the region uniquely and strategically prominent in the center of the American continent. It is that particularity of the Caribbean that European powers sought to exploit in earlier centuries. This resulted in the balkanization of the region, so that even today its generic significance is not always recognized.

The advent of the Spanish, British, French, and Dutch colonial powers in the Caribbean induced its political and economic fragmentation (but, significantly, colonialism also introduced a type of multilateralism) that turned the Caribbean away from itself and the Americas toward the European continent. Therefore, a Caribbean perception of itself as a geopolitical unit was not contextually conceivable. Each isolated entity saw its future development linked more to Europe than to the Western Hemisphere. Progressively, the British, French, Dutch, Spanish, and American Caribbean became engulfed in a wave of centrifugal configuration not conducive to regional cooperation and integration. Major constitutional changes in the Caribbean following World War II further institutionalized this separatism. The French colonies were assimilated constitutionally as overseas departments of France in 1946; the Dutch colonies associated in a special tripartite relationship with the Kingdom of the Netherlands in 1954; there was a federation of the British West Indies from 1958 to 1962; and following the independence of Jamaica and Trinidad and Tobago in 1962, the other British colonies moved quickly toward establishing their own political sovereignty.

These constitutional changes, especially in the former British colonies, paved the way for the "Caribbean" (which by then came to refer to the insular Caribbean, plus the British, French, and Dutch territories on the coast of Latin America and Belize in Central America) to begin to pay greater attention to its geopolitical situation in relation to the rest of the hemisphere. This marked a turning point in Caribbean self-awareness and identity. The era of decolonization also influenced this new perception. Colonialism was seen to be neither politically nor economically correct and certainly not compatible with the concept of the "family of nations."

Nevertheless, the vestiges of colonialism lingered on, impeding the liberation of a genuinely comprehensive and integrated Caribbean multilateral perception and approach to its hemispheric identity. This is not to say that efforts were not made to bridge the historical, political, and economic divide of the past. Intermittent political voices were raised persistently for a single, comprehensive Caribbean destiny. Political vision at the time, however, gave way to political immediacy in an era of fledgling and competing political relationships. Wider Caribbean cooperation and a hemispheric vision would have to await the previous consolidation of a Caribbean ethos on the basis of subsequent political mutations and vicissitudes.

For a long time, the English-speaking Caribbean was the only manifest regional grouping of this Caribbean ethos. The formation of a Caribbean Free Trade Area (CARIFTA) and its successor, the Caribbean Economic Community (CARICOM), were the harbingers of this Caribbean "regionalism." Currently, it is the propagation of that Caribbean ethos, on the initiative of CARICOM, that is central to the establishment of the ACS. An historic review of this process toward a wider regionalism, as stimulated by the English-speaking Caribbean and CARICOM, is instructive.

The accession to independence of Jamaica and Trinidad and Tobago in 1962 and Barbados and Guyana in 1966 were significant steps toward the opening up of the English-speaking Caribbean to the hemisphere. Both Trinidad and Tobago and Jamaica sought and gained entry into the Organization of American States, in spite of lingering suspicions (by other members of the body) of the true nature of their independence because of their continued membership in the British Commonwealth. Barbados subsequently joined the OAS, while Guyana's application for membership was delayed by Charter provision because of its border dispute with Venezuela. The membership of these former British colonies in the OAS marked the beginning of a trend that was to be followed by all the newly independent former British Caribbean territories. Membership in the OAS not only added a political dimension to their recognized geographical affiliation to the hemisphere but also introduced them to the economic, cultural, linguistic, institutional, juridical, and social diversities characteristic of hemispheric realities.

Accession to independence for these four British colonies also meant their introduction into the wider family of nations as they sought membership in the United Nations. Within the region, the perspective and conviction of a Caribbean identity within the United Nations Economic Commission for Latin America (ECLA), which included the Caribbean, led members of CARICOM to promote a revised nomenclature to that body explicitly including the Caribbean. Accordingly, the Commission was renamed the United Nations Economic Commission for Latin America and the Caribbean (ECLAC). CARICOM members further brought about the upgrading of the Port of Spain Office of ECLA to a subregional headquarters of ECLAC. They also institutionalized the Caribbean Development and Cooperation Committee (CDCC) to serve as a policy body for developmental questions in a wider Caribbean perspective. Its membership included Cuba, the Dominican Republic, Haiti, Suriname, Aruba, Puerto Rico, and the United States Virgin Islands, altogether twenty-two countries with a total population of approximately twenty-eight million people.

These initiatives at the international and hemispheric levels, as well as significant efforts to establish bilateral relations with Cuba, the Dominican Republic, and Haiti at very tumultuous and politically sensitive periods of their relations with the United States, were signs that the English-speaking Caribbean region had the potential to exploit its political neutrality and to play a significant role in hemispheric developments. However, to do this effectively, the imperative of an integrated approach to economic development saw the evolution of CARICOM as the genesis of true Caribbean multilateralism and the springboard of any significant effort toward a Caribbean perspective in hemispheric relations.

Bridging the Hemispheric Divide:
CARICOM Initiatives

The end of the Federation of the West Indies in 1962 did not daunt the hopes of the English-speaking Caribbean for some form of cooperation toward the strengthening of their internal relations, as well as for the emergence of a united force toward greater hemispheric and international relevance. The geopolitical configuration of the former British colonies favored the establishment of CARICOM as a fairly homogenous unit, notwithstanding the potential for internal problems deriving from differences in the levels of development of the member states. In the context of volatile hemispheric tensions in the 1970s, economic recession and debt at the international level in the 1980s, and the trade expansion and liberalization policies (which in 1990 prepared the introduction of the global economy of the twenty-first century), CARICOM continued through on its initiative to foster the cohesiveness of the region and to ensure the incremental development of relations with all countries of the hemisphere.

Established eleven years after Cuba was suspended from the OAS in January 1962, CARICOM sought to keep open the lines of communication with other Caribbean countries, notwithstanding their political ideologies. An historic example of this was the establishment in the early 1970s of diplomatic relations with Cuba by Trinidad and Tobago, Jamaica, Barbados, and Guyana despite Cuba's suspension from the OAS. The existence of these bilateral relations further contributed to the promotion of a continuing Caribbean outreach. Subsequently, CARICOM went even further and established joint technical cooperation with Cuba, Haiti, and the Dominican Republic. Another positive step in intra-Caribbean relations was facilitated by the significant role played by CARICOM in the negotiations of LOMÉ I in 1975, bringing the regional body into more direct contact with the French overseas departments and the Dutch territories in the region. These and other developments strengthened CARICOM in its outreach to the larger hemisphere.

The emerging global recession during the 1970s and 1980s mandated new initiatives for economic growth on the part of developing countries. The particular circumstances of CARICOM, with its limited economic resources and absence of a critical mass, compelled a vanguard approach to regional hemispheric penetration. In 1979, the San José Accord was signed by twenty-three Latin American and Caribbean countries. This multilateral Caribbean-Latin American arrangement for the creation and strengthening of mechanisms for increased cooperation, especially in the areas of energy, trade, and transport, set the foundation for the deepening of bilateral relations between Latin American and Caribbean countries. Simultaneously, multilateral cooperation was given a further significant boost by the membership of certain CARICOM member states in the Latin American Economic System (SELA) established in 1975 and headquartered in Caracas, Venezuela.

In 1982, Colombia and CARICOM issued a joint communiqué relative to the strengthening of relations with CARICOM member states in order to assure that the weaker Caribbean economies were not unfairly disadvantaged in their trade agreements with larger countries. In both the Nassau Understanding of 1984 and the Tobago Communiqué of 1989, CARICOM heads of state placed importance on the deepening of cooperation with Latin American states, as well as with integration movements in both subregions. CARICOM has since spearheaded a variety of follow-up meetings, arrangements, and technical forums in view of deepening relations with Brazil, Colombia, Venezuela, and Mexico and has played and continues to play a determinant role in current hemispheric trade issues. In all these negotiations, CARICOM has been, for the small Caribbean states, a watchdog for issues on asymmetrical reciprocity, trade integration and partnership, and the maintenance of effective provisions that recognize the particular circumstances of these small states. In the process of hemispheric integration, the CARICOM countries of the OAS have played a major role. They were very effective in having the Charter of the OAS amended at the Fifteenth Special Session of the General Assembly held in Washington, D.C., on January 8, 1991, by which Belize and Guyana gained admission to the Organization, and the principle of universality of membership was established in this hemispheric body.

The role of CARICOM in the mutual subregional outreach with Central America is also significant. It is perhaps best exemplified by the establishment of an institutional consultative mechanism between CARICOM and Central America. The first of such meetings was held in San Pedro Sula, Honduras, in 1992, followed by a second meeting in Kingston, Jamaica, and subsequent periodic meetings. This mechanism of consultation has as its principal objective the establishment of cooperation links between the two subregions as a basis for mutual economic development, cultural exchanges, and overall wider regional policy formulation. The implications for regional outreach and the consequent multilateral action are implicit in this joint subregional approach and underlie another important role developed by CARICOM for hemispheric collaboration and cooperation. Of particular significance is the increasing cooperative development between the government of Chile and many CARICOM member states. This joint initiative has opened up new possibilities and expanded vistas of hemispheric relations, given the current, unprecedented dynamics of subregional integration.

It is this double imperative of intra-Caribbean development priorities and the dynamism of global trade expansion and liberalization that also pushed CARICOM to spearhead the bold initiative for the creation of the

Association of Caribbean States (ACS). Timely and pragmatic as it may be, the ACS raises a number of questions about the future of Caribbean relations and the role of CARICOM and, in the context of the global transformations taking place, concern for the future sovereignty of the mini-CARICOM states at a time when economics might determine the ratio of dependence-independence. For the moment, however, multilateralism increasingly is shaping the character and future of the Caribbean Basin, and the Caribbean of the twenty-first century will be significantly different in terms of its geopolitical and economic realities.

In sum, the opening of the Caribbean to the rest of the hemisphere is the result of the Caribbean leadership's commitment (within and without CARICOM) to the benefits of regionalism and awareness of the evolving international political and economic circumstances, making a regional approach mandatory for further effective, pragmatic, and inevitable integration of the Caribbean into the world economy. As the international political and economic systems become progressively transformed and competitively integrated, countries of the Caribbean are compelled to strengthen their own regional economic and political integration, facilitate their hemispheric integration, and try to ensure their integration into the political and economic scenarios that are shaping the twenty-first century's world economic order.

However, the entire Caribbean is not yet served by such a perspective of Caribbean hemispheric cooperation. The French overseas departments in the region still approach their development from the perspective of priorities and perceptions established by the European Union. The former colonies of Holland in the Caribbean also pay attention to European priorities that are heavily determined by strict economic imperatives rather than by purely hemispheric policy considerations. Yet perceptions are changing, and a larger Caribbean is emerging.

Multilateralism in Caribbean Development

For the newly independent Caribbean states, their small size, mini-economies, and absence of critical mass were fundamental in their exploration of the possibilities of a multilateral approach to development needs. In 1993, the then-thirteen member countries of CARICOM,[1] with a total population of approximately 5.9 million and a total gross domestic product (GDP) at market prices of approximately $14.08 billion,[2] together with the rest of the insular Caribbean, Belize, Guyana, Suriname, and French Guyana, comprised a total area of 752,980 square kilometers. Collectively, these countries represent a very small market by world standards, and their trading potential does not compare with any of the other hemispheric subgroupings in existence. Given these circumstances, multilateralism is an evolving international economic requisite that informs and impels a Caribbean perspective of its development and hemispheric involvement. In the Preamble of the Treaty establishing the Caribbean Community, the principle of seeking complementarity in the multilateral approach rather than in competitive national interests is clearly expressed:

> The Governments of the Contracting States, determined to consoli-date and strengthen the bonds which have historically existed among their peoples;

> Sharing a common determination to fulfill the hopes and aspirations of their peoples for full employment and improved standards of work and living;

> Conscious that these objectives can most rapidly be attained by the optimum utilization of available human and natural resources of the Region to accelerated, coordinated, and sustained economic devel-opment, particularly through the exercise of permanent sovereignty over their natural resources; by the efficient operation of common services and functional cooperation in social, cultural, educational, and technological fields; and by a common front in relation to the external world; convinced of the need to elaborate an effective regime by establishing and utilizing institutions designed to enhance the economic, social, and cultural development of their peoples.[3]

Over the years, CARICOM has sought to deepen its integration process through the broadening of functional cooperation in a wide range of areas. But as one approaches the twenty-first century when the global tendency is toward establishing a global market, while at the same time expanding open regionalism in order to secure a greater and fairer share of that market, the Caribbean needs more and more to come to terms with the new circumstances and exploit the realities of its hemispheric presence. Hemispheric integration for economic, social, and integrated development is the only way the Caribbean can avoid marginalization in a progressively integrated interna-tional environment.

The Caribbean Contribution to Multilateralism

The historical links between the Caribbean and Europe did not prevent the opening of the entire subregion (with the exception of the French departments) to increasing trade and immigration links with the North American countries of Canada and the United States. Thousands of Caribbean nationals live and work in the United States and Canada, and both these countries have offered preferential trading arrangements and most-favored nation (MFN) preferences to Caribbean countries. But apart from these arrangements that have served CARICOM member countries with varying degrees of effectiveness and apart from the traditional links between the Spanish Caribbean and Latin America, the Caribbean, as a whole, is a relatively new player at the hemispheric level.

Besides the economic benefits to be derived from a multilateral approach to its relations with the hemisphere and the obvious impact on the integral development of member countries, the Caribbean as a region can make an important contribution to the objectives of hemispheric cooperation. The goals of such cooperation were expressed clearly at the Summit of the Americas held in Miami in December 1994. They are threefold: to extend and establish hemisphere-wide free trade, to strengthen the democratic process in all the countries of the hemisphere, and to improve the quality of life of all citizens. The potential of the Caribbean to contribute to such hemisphere-wide partnership should not be minimized. In CARICOM, the Caribbean possesses a fairly homogenous and stable regional body that has begun to serve as a nucleus for the expansion of multilateral subregional outreach and, at the same time, as a vehicle for the consolidation and broadening of the region's cooperation with the rest of the hemisphere. The West Indian Commission recognized this urgency in its report:

> ...CARICOM should remain the inner core of our relationship in the Region, and...we should consciously create space beyond member-ship of CARICOM for development of CARICOM's integrationist relationships with Caribbean countries from Central America to Suriname, from Cuba to Venezuela.[4]

As a region, the Caribbean brings to hemispheric outreach its very important cultural and linguistic diversity, its highly gifted and literate human resources, and, through its historical links with Europe, the potential to explore broader cross-hemispheric cooperation for development. The relatively stable and continuous practice of democracy in the Caribbean CARICOM countries also constitutes an important base on which to build and institutionalize democracy as a way of life within the hemisphere.

The Caribbean and the Organization of American States

Hemispheric cooperation in the Americas is by no means a recent phenomenon. Established in 1948 as the first hemispheric organization of its kind anywhere on the five continents, the Organization of American States is at the center of hemispheric cooperation. Founded on the basic principles aimed at strengthening peace, security, and development in the hemisphere through the pacific settlement of disputes, coordinated action against aggression, the common solution of problems among member states, and the promotion of cooperative action for development, the Organization has moved beyond the sectoral approach in responding to the priorities of member states as identified by their national governments. Through its experiences over the years, the Organization has been able to adapt to the changing circumstances and needs of the hemisphere, and today the integral approach to development is stipulated clearly in the revised Charter of the Organization. Article 30 of Chapter 6 of the Charter states,

> Inter-American cooperation for integral development is the common and joint responsibility of Member States, within the framework of the democratic principles of the institutions of the inter-American System. It should include the economic, social, educational, cultural, scientific, and technological fields, support achievement of national objectives of the Member States, and respect the priorities established by each country in the development plans, without political ties or conditions.

The objective of cooperation for integral development touches at the heart of the development objectives of Caribbean member states in a world where the compartmentalization of knowledge, skills, and projects in development is a thing of the past. The technological innovations that constantly are taking place, especially in the field of communications, already have begun and continue to change the way we work and the way we live. Today, competence and efficiency in one field necessitate knowledge of a wide range of other areas if one is to be marketable in this highly competitive society. The emphasis on integral development, therefore, reflects the understanding of member states of the hemisphere of the evolving challenges to development that the new circumstances impose. It is an approach that can be described as multisectoral in a multilateral context.

All independent Caribbean nations are now members of theOAS. Today, CARICOM states in the Organization number thirteen, not an insignificant number in a total membership of thirty-five. Given its relatively stable democracies and accountability in governance, CARICOM within the Organization emphasizes technical cooperation and economic cooperation. In May 1992, the Caribbean Community and the General Secretariat of the Organization of American States signed the Nassau Agreement for the development of cooperative relations, in conformity with Article 117(h) of the Charter of the OAS. This agreement covers cooperation and consultation between both bodies on areas of common interest, consistent with their respective objectives. This has resulted in the OAS granting technical assistance to CARICOM in such areas as tax harmonization, economic and social affairs, business, employment creation, trade, and multilateral expansion for the creation and development of the ACS. The First General Meeting of CARICOM and the OAS was held in Georgetown, Guyana, on March 22-23, 1995. It was an historic occasion and signaled a turning point in Caribbean-hemispheric relations. It represents a new multilateral thrust to the region's hemispheric cooperation and will serve also to facilitate the movement toward total hemispheric integration with the creation of the Free Trade Area of the Americas by the year 2005.

Hemispheric free trade will necessitate cooperation in a wide range of other areas, among which environmental issues, technology and industrialization, legislative procedures, standardization, the environment, services, social development, and education are just a few of the crucial sectors. If CARICOM explores the multilateral perspective of development in these areas within the context of the hemispheric body, it already will be paving the way to strengthen its position in the great hemispheric commercial endeavor scheduled for the year 2005, which, most certainly, will be the main thrust of twenty-first century hemispheric relations.

Given these identified priorities, a number of questions need to be addressed in order to understand better the hemispheric and international circumstances that make them mandatory. Two such questions are 1) what makes these issues important, and how far is a Caribbean multilateral approach to confronting them the best possible response; and 2) should a particularly Caribbean approach be explored apart from or within the wider hemispheric agenda? Answers to these questions will serve not only to shed further light on the constraints to Caribbean development but also to extend further the region's perspective of multilateralism in the hemispheric context that recently was given a significant boost by the creation of the ACS in July 1994.

The issues themselves can be grouped under four main headings: the environment, politics and governance, economics, and social development. The environment, as a factor of development, has assumed national and international importance during these last decades of the twentieth century and in the future will demand increasing attention. Concern for the preservation of the ozone layer and for the effects of acid rain are two of the many factors that, together with natural disasters, have demonstrated how fragile and certainly far from being inexhaustible our natural environment resource is. Our greater understanding of the value of the earth's ecosystems to our survival at the human, social, and economic levels has encouraged a reevaluation of our attitudes to environmental issues. In the Caribbean in particular, where mineral resources are limited and where the importance of the resource potential of the natural environment cannot be overestimated, there is need for a policy for proper and effective management in this area in order to maximize its contribution to development, prevent the indiscriminate use and abuse of environmental resources, and minimize the occurrence and effects of natural disasters. The Earth Summit held in Brazil in 1992, under the auspices of the United Nations, has been the highest level of multilateral cooperation in that area that has stressed the need for continued multilateral collaboration for the preservation of our natural environment.

In the Caribbean region, the environment is at the center of the tourism industry, which is the principal source of revenue for most countries, and coordination in the tourism sector inevitably implies coordination in the area of the environment. In the context of the new hemispheric outreach, current intra-CARICOM coordination on environmental issues enables the region to be part of any efforts to collaborate at the hemispheric level. A number of factors prescribe a Caribbean multilateral perspective on hemispheric cooperation on environmental issues. Fortunately, the region has reached the stage of expressing regret about its political and economic dissection by colonial powers. One unquestionable factor has been the region's inviolability as a geographical unit, meaning that the destruction of one part affects the whole. It is, therefore, evident that a Caribbean multilateral perspective in all areas related to the environment is as natural as the environment itself. Any other interpretation would constitute an anomaly. What is true at the subregional level also applies for the entire hemisphere, and OAS/CARICOM collaboration on the environment and related issues becomes especially significant. The urgent needs for effective disaster emergency response, lifeline vulnerability reduction, storm hazard assessment and impact monitoring, disaster preparedness and prevention, related insurances, environmental health and population relocation — all constitute issues of priority concern throughout the hemisphere. For CARICOM, consensus and collaboration at the regional level could be but one arm of the entire regional drive.

The Caribbean can be described as the only region in the world that harbors such diverse political, administrative, and institutional systems in such a small area with such a limited total population. Historical fragmentation into Spanish, English, French, Dutch, and, more recently, American systems of politics and governance testifies to the plurality of constraints that collaboration in these areas would have to confront. However, whatever the system in existence, the professed objectives continue to be the establishment of the highest levels of justice, democracy, and well-being for all.

A difficult situation does not necessarily mean that there are no solutions, and if local regional imperatives for collaboration in these areas do not prevail, the international and hemispheric circumstances will dictate other responses. Recent events in Haiti serve as a classic example of how the internal abuse of democracy and justice in one country can impact not only on its own economic and entire developmental drive but also on the stability and security of the region. The concerted and measured response of CARICOM to these events subsequently had an impact on the OAS and the United Nations. The situation was serious enough to solicit widespread international collaboration, and it was only as a "regional" entity that the Caribbean could play its part in any significant way. The formation of the ACS offers an opportunity for the extension of collaboration, both qualitatively and geographically, thus enhancing the multilateral Caribbean presence and impact on the promotion and enhancement of good governance, democracy, human rights, and justice in the region.

In any truly democratic society, there will be an almost natural correlation between economic development and the growth of a just social order and well-being for all citizens. A more widespread distribution of the nation's resources will be created, thus reducing the possibility of growing social and economic imbalances. In this era of globalization, not only in economic terms but also in the areas of social development, this same correlation (economic-social) applies at other levels, be they regional, hemispheric, or international. An illustrative example is the complex issue of drug trafficking. In the context of continuing abject poverty in some countries, created by an international economic order that is manifestly imbalanced, the unscrupulous exploitation of drug abuse proliferates. The result is the further institutionalization of poverty in the poor countries, economic destabilization, and deterioration of global social values. With these issues in mind, OAS/CARICOM collaboration on economic and social issues is fundamental, not only to Caribbean development but also to proper positioning of the region in a hemispheric drive for the fulfillment of the hemispheric responsibilities and commitments reemphasized by the Summit of the Americas. For the subregion, the development and strengthening of the multilateral approach in this area could only be interpreted as the region positioning itself to maximize both its contribution to and benefits from the current hemispheric outreach. The wide range of sectors to be covered in each major area are indicative of the extent and importance of the reforms and developments to be carried out. It is a very complex system of intersectoral and cross-sectoral linkages that the following diagram seeks to illustrate:

Economic	**Social**
Hemispheric Free Trade	Education, Science, Culture
Caribbean Central American Relations	Drugs
Economic Development	Epidemiology
Tourism	Information System
	Public Education
	Law Enforcement

As the diagram indicates, the issues are interrelated and cannot be dealt with effectively in isolation. Viewed also from a more central perspective, the interrelated nature of these issues becomes more comprehensive and the planned strategies to be adopted more consequential. In this new configuration, nurtured by Caribbean multilateral perception of the benefits to be derived and the constraints to be overcome, the region will be setting the stage for the strengthening of its position at all levels of hemispheric outreach.

Strengthening Subregional Multilateralism in the Hemisphere: The Case of the ACS

The drive for the creation of an Association of Caribbean States, bringing together all those countries and territories historically and geographically Caribbean, was initiated and encouraged by CARICOM in the vital search for deeper and expanded relations with the rest of the hemisphere. However, the same imperatives that mandated the formation of CARICOM itself in 1973 are today much more acute because of the new international and hemispheric circumstances that are shaping the priorities and strategies for the twenty-first century. Since the formation of CARICOM two decades ago, the world has changed a great deal. The political hostilities between East and West have been defused; the European Union is rapidly consolidating its perception of an economically and politically powerful Europe, free of colonial responsibilities, within an integrated world economy; and major economies on the American continent are seeking to parallel the European move. Increasingly, the politics of trade and economic issues, facilitated by innovations in the field of communications technology, have brought to smaller states and groups of states the realization of their worsening vulnerability unless they face the future in association with other states. In the Caribbean, CARICOM faces the precarious position where the conflict of historical realities and present-day circumstances forces them to change their own perceptions, conditioned by the realities of the American continent rather than those shaping developments in Europe. It becomes necessary for the regional grouping to be integrated into the hemisphere in unprecedented ways.

The broadening and deepening of Caribbean multilateralism to include the larger and culturally diverse countries of Central America, Cuba, the Dominican Republic, Haiti, Venezuela, Colombia, and Mexico, above and beyond questions of shades of ideological differences, is but a first step toward full hemispheric integration of Caribbean Basin countries, as envisioned by the establishment of the ACS. With a total population of 204 million and an accumulated GDP of $508 billion, the ACS has the potential to be a significant economic force and, in a world where economic issues have assumed much political importance, a significant political force as well. The ACS is poised to exploit its potential as one of the world's largest subregional groupings with a total export trade of $80 billion and an import trade of $100 billion. The initial common objective of the ACS in addressing common trade problems related to transportation links, trade, and tourism is just a first step along the road to the forging of closer economic, social, and, inevitably, political links between CARICOM and other Caribbean states and territories. The first successful ACS

Summit held in Trinidad on August 22-23, 1995, was therefore an historic moment for the furtherance of a timely Caribbean presence in inter-hemispheric relations.

In the context of the trade and economic objectives of the ACS whose members face a number of constraints in respect to variations in size, economies, and levels of development, there are three important factors that should be noted. The first is that the ACS is seeking to chart a course at the same time that two important economic movements are taking shape in the hemisphere: the great project of hemispheric free trade by 2005 and the creation of a North American Free Trade Area. The parallelism in the development of these initiatives affords the ACS an opportunity to play a significant role in this historic hemispheric economic movement. The second important factor is that the significant presence of the OAS members within the ACS affords an opportunity to revisit the hemispheric relationship with Cuba as a member of the ACS, in the context of economics, politics, and consolidated Caribbean integration. The third factor concerns the Latin American element of the ACS, which consists of over 80 percent of the population of that Caribbean body. CARICOM member countries traditionally have had closer and more intricate links with the North American countries of Canada and the United States than with Latin America. The ACS today represents potentially the most direct and intense level of cooperation between CARICOM and Latin American countries individually and collec-tively. Existing economic differences might, therefore, be engaged effectively at a level of political comity that might not have been possible previously. If this political circumstance is managed effectively, the ACS well might become a solid multilateral mechanism on which to base the deepening of Caribbean hemispheric relations.

Multilateralism for the Twenty-first Century

Many of the persistent problems facing the global community elude the goodwill of leaders and policymakers to find lasting solutions, since in many instances they seem not to have accepted fully that traditional approaches, conditioned by predominantly national interests, are incompat-ible with the trends toward multilateralism that are progressively shaping our introduction into the twenty-first century. In the Americas, for example, there are three major problems facing the entire hemisphere:

1. The environment as a critical factor in sustainable development;

2. Persistent poverty, even among certain sections of the population of the more affluent countries; and

3. The development of the drug problem to almost epidemic propor-tions.

It is becoming increasingly clear that no amount of time and money spent to combat the drug problem in North America, or elsewhere in the world for that matter, will bear any significant results unless they are linked to projects aimed at eliminating persistent poverty in Latin America and the continued marginalization of large sections of the world's population and, in the particular case of the Americas, at significantly advancing programs for the integral development of all citizens. The increasing interdependence of the world economy results in the progressive establishment of an international community marked by shared sovereignty in an international context, where the exercise of individual national sovereignty in many areas of national life is becoming more and more difficult. This, in turn, requires prudence, circumspection, and consultation in the consideration of unilateral decisions on many sensitive issues. Multilateralism as a function of global relations continues to shape trends and responses in the international community, in relation to the factors and constraints of development, through a movement to expand and deepen relations with other states that have shared priorities and objectives. It is in response to these imperatives, and consistent with current trends, that the Caribbean Basin countries have broadened their association from a fourteen-member CARICOM integration movement by the formation of the twenty-five-member Association of Caribbean States. The ACS, whatever its initial mandates, inevitably must be a platform for more effective relations between the Caribbean and the hemisphere. In this overall regional configuration, all players stand to benefit from the expansion of multilateralism through new associations with neighboring countries and regions. In the case of the Caribbean and its relations with the hemisphere, certain factors make this perspective even more crucial.

Conclusion

A cademics and politicians agree that trade development, whether it be in goods or services, is the single most important imperative for economic and social advancement. However, in the absence of sufficient levels of development in some of the very areas targeted, trade cannot develop, and economic growth will be stunted accordingly. In this regard, financial stability, sufficient levels of social security, health (including the environment), education, and political stability coupled with national credibility are crucial elements in the developmental construct. The contextual limitations of the Caribbean countries, in terms of their size, economies, population, social development, and security as they can be variedly applied, require certain strategies for the successful management of trade-related matters. Social and economic asymmetry in the region, therefore, make interdependence an important element of the regional agenda — an agenda that is inscribed in the broader hemispheric outreach for free trade by the year 2005. The multilateral perspective in Caribbean hemispheric relations is strategically sound insofar as it concerns the future development of the Caribbean. The region will make even greater strides if this movement is made to include the wider forum of social partners influencing regional development.

The wider Caribbean ethos is increasingly on the rise. This ethos, beginning with the Caribbean Community, has radiated outwards to engage the CARICOM/Central American mechanism, the CARICOM bilateralism with other countries of the subregion, and more recently a larger Association of Caribbean States. The catalytic initiative of CARICOM in this development is a matter of record. However, the ACS is not an end in itself. It must contribute (in complementarity with other hemispheric and subregional bodies) to a wider multilateralism on the basis of consolidated functional cooperation and a general framework of political comity. This framework must be based on a recognition of the interdependence of countries of the region and the development of shared sovereignty in vital areas of hemispheric advancement and overall integration.

Notes

1. Suriname acceded to membership in 1995.

2. Based on Statistics of the CARICOM Secretariat.

3. *Treaty Establishing the Caribbean Community. Chaguaramas, Trinidad and Tobago, July 4, 1973.* Georgetown, Guyana: CARICOM Secretariat.

4. *Overview of the Report of the West Indian Commission,* Barbados, 1992, 67.

References

The Association of Caribbean States (ACS) - A Commentary. 1994. UN ECLAC/CDCC General, LC/CAR/G.425, July 13, 12 pages.

ECLAC. 1984. *El Regionalismo Abierto en América Latina y el Caribe.* La Integración Económica al Servicio de la Transformación Productiva con Equidad. Santiago de Chile: Comisión Económica para América Latina y el Caribe, 109 pages.

Latin American and Caribbean Relations. 1992. Revised version of Paper LC/G.1725 (Ses. 24/17) ECLAC/Distr. GENERAL, LC/CAR/G.379, November 18, 27 pages.

Report of the First General Meeting of the Caribbean Community (CARICOM) and the Organization of American States (OAS). 1995. Georgetown, Guyana: Caribbean Community, March 22-23, 33 pages.

Time for Action - The Report of the West Indian Commission. 1992. Black Rock, Christ Church, Barbados: The West Indian Commission, 591 pages.

Treaty Establishing the Caribbean Community. Chaguaramas, Trinidad and Tobago, July 4, 1973. Georgetown, Guyana: CARICOM Secretariat.

Chapter Six

Widening the Relationship?
The Association of Caribbean States

Henry S. Gill

Introduction

Over the last five years or so, many governments in Latin America and the Caribbean have expressed concern about the proliferation of intergovernmental organizations in the region, which are frequently assumed to have an unnecessary overlapping and even duplication of responsibilities. Notwithstanding this concern, a new body has recently appeared amid the already complicated institutional constellation. The convention establishing the Association of Caribbean States (ACS) was signed in Cartagena, Colombia, on July 24, 1994 — a highly symbolic date, marking the birthday of the Liberator, Simón Bolívar.

The signing ceremony was attended by heads of state and government, ministers of foreign affairs, and other representatives of twenty-four of the twenty-five states in and around the Caribbean Sea that are eligible for full ACS membership. Only El Salvador was not a signatory at Cartagena but is reportedly now ready to become one. France also signed as an associate member on behalf of Martinique, Guadeloupe, and Guyane. The convention will enter into force upon deposit of instruments of ratification by two-thirds of the states eligible for full membership.

The establishment of the ACS undoubtedly marks a highly ambitious attempt at bringing together peoples and economies of Caribbean Basin "states, countries, and territories," in the wording of the convention, because of the 1) considerable variation in geographic, demographic, and economic size and development levels; 2) dissimilar historical, cultural, and linguistic backgrounds; and 3) different constitutional statuses, embracing sovereign and nonindependent territories. (The French overseas depart-

This chapter was previously published as "Association of Caribbean States: Prospects for a 'Quantum Leap,'" *North-South Agenda Paper 11* (January 1995). Coral Gables, Fla.: University of Miami North-South Center Press.

ments in the Caribbean form perhaps a category apart, since they are said to share in the common sovereignty of France.) The timing of this event is noteworthy in at least one important respect: it coincides with ongoing conflict between producers covered by the Banana Protocol of the Lomé Convention and the so-called "dollar producers" over access for bananas to the European Union (EU).

Not surprisingly, this effort to integrate such heterogeneous units has been referred to as the boldest Caribbean undertaking ever, aimed at reversing the course of the area's history of separation and divisiveness. The Secretary-General of the Caribbean Community (CARICOM) regards the ACS as potentially constituting a "quantum leap" in the development of closer regional collaboration and integration; others wonder whether it will become another institution that promises much but delivers little.

This paper seeks to examine critically what has been created in order to gauge the prospects of the association. It traces the evolution of the ACS initiative from the origin of the idea, then assesses the interests of the potential membership, and explains the process leading to the signing of the convention. Second, it explains the nature of the association by summarizing the main provisions of the convention, and it offers some insights into the association's possible thrust by outlining a number of elements that could be included in the initial ACS work program. Third, it examines six areas of challenge that the eventual membership needs to resolve if the association is to grapple successfully with its task. Some concluding remarks are then made concerning the possible outlook for the ACS.

Evolution of an Initiative

Genesis

S ignificantly, the ACS initiative originated in the English-speaking Caribbean, connoting an important shift toward a proactive approach to collaboration with their non-Anglophone neighbors in the Caribbean Basin. The speed with which the process has developed serves to demonstrate as well that much larger neighbors can be responsive to a project of this magnitude launched from the Caribbean Community.

The ACS idea was one of the most salient recommendations contained in the 1992 report of the West Indian Commission entitled *Time for Action*. The commission had been set up by the CARICOM heads of government, under the chairmanship of Sir Shridath Ramphal, former secretary-general of the Commonwealth Secretariat in London, in order to recommend appropriate directions and changes for their societies in approaching the twenty-first century. Toward this end, broad-based consultations were undertaken with

West Indians as the commission traveled throughout the Community and beyond. The authors of the report recognized that their Community of 5.5 million people was obviously too small to meet the challenges of an increasingly competitive international environment successfully on its own. As a result, they sought to find a way for CARICOM to remain intact as a grouping and yet operate within a larger economic space.

The ACS idea was adopted by a special meeting of the Conference of Heads of Government of the Caribbean Community, held in Port of Spain, Trinidad and Tobago, in October 1992. The conference agreed that CARICOM should "seek to bridge the divide between its member states and other states and territories of the Caribbean and Latin America" and recognized the advent of an increasingly "Caribbean Basin" approach to international negotiations and development issues, as well as the changes within and among Latin American countries. The conference decided that CARICOM would initiate proposals for the establishment of an ACS to advance *both economic integration and functional cooperation* with the other Caribbean Basin countries. The conference also determined that the ACS would be open to all CARICOM member states, the other island states of the Caribbean, Suriname, the states of Central America, and the Latin American countries of the Caribbean littoral and would allow for a variety of arrangements appropriate to its membership.[1]

The ACS idea was taken a step further through discussions of the newly created bureau of CARICOM,[2] at its first meeting in December 1992, which proposed clear guidelines for orienting the objectives and work of the association in these terms:

> The Association should be seen as a grouping of states that would focus its activities on a selected range of important issues that will help to define the association itself and would enable the ACS to develop intra-Caribbean Basin cooperation, and as a group to adopt common guidelines for engaging in international dialogue.[3]

The bureau also endorsed the following program activities for immediate focus:

- Intra-group trade liberalization and trade promotion;
- Functional cooperation in such areas as energy, the sea bed, the environment, higher and tertiary education, culture, drug abuse abatement and control, language training, agricultural and industrial development, and transportation and communications; and
- Development and cooperation of a group relationship with the rest of the hemisphere, for example, with regard to the North American Free Trade Agreement (NAFTA).

Potential

Based on the definition provided by the CARICOM conference, twenty-five Caribbean Basin states are eligible to be full members: Antigua and Barbuda, the Bahamas, Barbados, Belize, Colombia, Costa Rica, Cuba, Dominica, the Dominican Republic, El Salvador, Grenada, Guatemala, Guyana, Haiti, Honduras, Jamaica, Nicaragua, Panama, St. Kitts and Nevis, St. Lucia, St. Vincent and the Grenadines, Suriname, Trinidad and Tobago, United States of Mexico, and Venezuela.

In addition, the following countries and territories are eligible for associate status: Anguilla, Bermuda, British Virgin Islands, Cayman Islands, Montserrat, Puerto Rico, Turks and Caicos Islands, United States Virgin Islands, the French Republic (in respect to Guadeloupe, Guyane, and Martinique), and the Kingdom of the Netherlands (on behalf of Aruba and the Netherlands Antilles).

Together the population of these "states, countries, and territories" exceeds 200 million, with an accumulated gross domestic product (GDP) surpassing $500 billion, as shown in Table 1. This can represent a very significant collectivity, and has been promoted as the world's fourth-largest economic grouping, but it must be noted that the G-3 countries (Colombia, Mexico, and Venezuela) constitute 67 percent of this population and 78 percent of GDP.

Still, the ACS is potentially a more significant grouping than either MERCOSUR or the Andean Pact but much smaller than certain others, particularly in respect to trading strength, as Table 2 indicates. Its membership possesses *inter alia* very significant energy resources (petroleum, coal, and hydroelectricity), important bauxite reserves, as well as nickel, gold, diamonds, and other raw materials.

Interests of CARICOM Countries

The ACS represents a sharp departure from traditional CARICOM integration scenarios, which have centered on the dichotomy of the "widening" and "deepening" of CARICOM. These options are regarded not merely as interdependent but crucially also as antithetical, the integration challenge consequently being presented as "the widening versus the deepening" of CARICOM. It was long argued that both options could not be pursued simultaneously, since opening CARICOM membership to non-Commonwealth Caribbean countries would dilute group homogeneity and therefore jeopardize chances of deepening the integration process. Accordingly, to follow the argument, widening would have to await deepening.

Table 1.
Comparisons Among ACS Groups ($US millions)

Groups of Countries	Population (Thousands)	GDP (Millions)	Exports (Millions)	Imports (Millions)
Caribbean	35,280	81,196	26,539	41,231
CARICOM	5,655	15,704	3,185	6,575
Non-CARICOM	25,122	24,013	2,248	5,396
Non-independent Territories	4,503	11,479	21,106	29,261
Central America	29,960	28,112	4,763	7,731
Group of Three (G-3)	136,837	399,090	49,585	52,820
ACS Total	*202,077*	*508,398*	*80,883*	*101,782*

Source: Compiled by the Centro de Investigación Económica para el Caribe (CIECA), Santo Domingo.

Table 2.
Relative Size of the Association of Caribbean States

A Comparison of Key Social and Economic Indicators of Other Trade Areas with Those of the ACS (ACS level = 100%)

Grouping	Population	GNP	Exports	Imports
European Union	58.6%	8.4%	4.8%	5.3%
NAFTA	55.6%	8.2%	15.4%	15.2%
Asian Bloc	37.7%	13.8%	15.5%	18.5%
MERCOSUR	103.6%	106.0%	178.3%	358.9%
Andean Pact	119.5%	113.4%	145.3%	173.2%

Source: Prepared by CIECA.

But the problem is more complex. Widening has perhaps *sui generis* consequences for CARICOM, since nearly all actual or potential candidates for joining CARICOM (Cuba, Haiti, the Dominican Republic, and, more recently, Venezuela) are demographically larger than all Commonwealth Caribbean countries combined. This fact raises the specter of a shift in the center of gravity of the integration process away from CARICOM, not just economically but also politically and culturally. The compatibility of institutions and practices with those of CARICOM countries, which derived uniformly from a common colonial experience, was also a concern. Against this backdrop, consideration of the Dominican Republic's application for membership in the Caribbean Community had long been postponed, just as Haiti's before it. Venezuela's application was problematic: it was not clear how its membership in the Andean Pact could be reconciled with CARICOM obligations, since both groupings maintained different common external tariff structures. From a demographic and economic standpoint, Suriname could be a less problematic partner, but major political difficulties remained. In brief, the rub is that despite CARICOM's decision to implement a single market, little deepening was in fact taking place, and as deepening continued to be postponed so was widening.

The old argument of widening versus deepening is clearly no longer intellectually sustainable and can be empirically refuted. The European Union (EU) experience demonstrates that its expansion from nine to twelve members did not impede the progressive deepening of the unity process. Moreover, the ambitious goals of the Single Market and the Maastricht Treaty are being tackled amidst an impending new expansion of EU membership, with Austria, Finland, Norway (Norway voted "No" to membership in the EU in November 1994), and Sweden poised for accession by January 1, 1995. Such trends point to a recognition of the necessity for managing the simultaneous widening and deepening of integration processes, since present-day global competition requires an expansion of economic interaction spheres. If large economies treat this as an imperative, for small economies the requirement is even greater.

But the model followed is more akin to the European Economic Area, which came into effect from January 1, 1994, against which the real significance of the ACS decision can perhaps be more easily understood. The ACS decision marks a change of premise on the part of the leadership of CARICOM countries, and perhaps also a psychological shift. Whereas in the past it had been assumed, though never explicitly stated, that systematized interaction or integration with non-Commonwealth Caribbean countries could occur only through the latter's accession to CARICOM membership (which aroused concerns about compatibility and "indigestion"), the new approach is to create a wider economic space within which CARICOM would participate; CARICOM itself would remain intact, with eventually just one or two additions of lesser significance.[4]

Such an approach simultaneously caters to the requirement of a more broad-based regionalism and allays CARICOM apprehension; it also facilitates a CARICOM response to requests for membership by providing an alternative context for close interaction with geographically proximate neighbors.

Interests of Other Potential Members

The ACS proposal elicited from a very early stage a high degree of interest in at least two capitals — Havana and Santo Domingo — but it was less easy to gauge real interest elsewhere.

Cuba's leaders obviously saw an important opportunity for integration within its closest geographical area, which could help to reduce the country's isolation following the breakup of Comecon and the disintegration and re-orientation of the republics of the former Soviet Union. Membership in ACS could yield important political, economic, and other dividends for Cuba, particularly in terms of investment, tourism, and other trade areas. Cuban government representatives were active in urging speedier implementation of the ACS decision, considering it important to register their interest in getting the process moving, especially since the United States was working to preempt Cuban participation in the new body.

For somewhat similar reasons, the Joaquín Balaguer government in the Dominican Republic appeared excited by the prospect of ACS membership. Its December 1989 application for membership in the Caribbean Community had been placed on the CARICOM back burner,[5] but the Dominican Republic felt an increasing need to belong to an integration grouping amidst regional, hemispheric, and global trends which it interpreted as favoring group action. As the ACS decision was made known, the Dominican government established a national commission to study the subject and pave the way for the country's active participation in ACS deliberations. Early indication was given of the government's desire to host the headquarters of the new grouping.

By contrast, the regime in Haiti manifested no interest in joining the ACS, aware no doubt that the overthrow of the Aristide government made it politically unacceptable. On the other hand, President Jean-Bertrand Aristide, who had received strong support from CARICOM and other Caribbean Basin governments, particularly Venezuela, was represented at the various preparatory meetings.

The importance of the ACS initiative could hardly be lost on the Group of Three (Colombia, Mexico, and Venezuela), which had separately interacted closely with CARICOM and with Central American and other Caribbean Basin countries over a broad spectrum of cooperative activities and for which the

Caribbean Basin represents an area of strategic interest. A stated objective of the G-3 has also been the fostering of closer relations between CARICOM and Central American countries. An important milestone was passed in October 1993, when the G-3 jointly made public their support for the ACS idea. The occasion was a summit of the heads of state and government of the Caribbean Community, the G-3, and the vice president of Suriname, held in Port of Spain. The joint communiqué issued at the end of the summit confirmed a willingness to participate as full members in the association, which they saw as providing a permanent forum for dialogue and contributing to the process of economic integration and cooperation among "all the developing countries and territories of the Caribbean Basin."[6] This last seemingly innocuous phrase nevertheless confirmed that no "developed" country was being considered for ACS membership.[7]

The position of the Central American countries was initially less clear. The subject was discussed at the second meeting of the CARICOM and Central American Integration System (SIECA) secretariats, held in Guatemala City on February 15-16, 1993. On that occasion the CARICOM Secretary-General took the opportunity of informing the meeting about the ACS proposal,[8] in response to which the Central American side observed that there were many commonalties between the proposed ACS approach and their own position on expanding relations with the Caribbean. But there remained some uncertainty concerning the extent of real interest even after the Central American countries gave their support at the Second CARICOM/Central America Ministerial Conference, held in Kingston, Jamaica, in May 1993.

With respect to the non-sovereign entities, France demonstrated no little interest in the initiative and would later make clear its aspiration to full membership, resisting participation of its Caribbean departments in their own right. On the other hand, U.S. opposition to Cuba's eventual membership no doubt ensured the non-participation of both Puerto Rico and the U.S. Virgin Islands, while the Pedro Rossello government of Puerto Rico publicly argued that it preferred to await developments. Little indication of interest was forthcoming from either the Dutch or the British territories.

Process

Technical work at the CARICOM level began early in 1993, gaining momentum much later in the year with the setting up of an expert group whose work concluded in early 1994. In the interim, Michael Manley, former prime minister of Jamaica, had been chosen to carry out consultations with a number of countries, which yielded positive responses by all accounts. Activity at this stage was not limited to CARICOM, and seminars with regional participation were held in both the Dominican Republic and Venezuela. Consultations also took place at the Latin American Economic System (SELA) permanent secretariat in Caracas among representatives of potential ACS members.

By early 1994, the time seemed ripe for the start of the more broad-based process involving the non-CARICOM countries. The first technical meeting of the whole was held in Kingston, in March 1994, under the chairmanship of Ambassador Don Bryce of Jamaica, who had served as executive secretary to the West Indian Commission. He continued to chair subsequent meetings held in Santo Domingo (May), Mexico City (early June), and finally Caracas (late June), since it was decided that these were merely resumed sessions of a single, ongoing technical meeting. The Caracas meeting was immediately followed by a ministerial session attended primarily by foreign ministers, at the end of which a draft convention was approved and initialed. As indicated, this convention was subsequently signed at Cartagena de Indias on July 24, 1994.

In general, these meetings hardly debated different conceptualizations of the nature and character of the ACS. The orientation suggested in the documentation tabled by the CARICOM secretariat was easily accepted, taking what could be termed a traditional approach in proposing trade integration and functional cooperation, while some delegations might have had different preferences. Mexico, for example, had indicated privately that the concept it preferred was an Organization for Economic Cooperation and Development (OECD)-type body, but this was never tabled as a proposal.

This situation may have arisen in a context in which the larger countries were somewhat reluctant to give any appearance of wanting to dominate or even influence too heavily the trend of discussions, preferring instead to allow CARICOM countries to get their views across. The problem is that CARICOM countries had not considered alternative conceptual models, nor had they come to the meetings with fully considered positions on all aspects of their own overall proposal. Similarly, there was little discussion of how precise objectives were to be tackled in achieving the broad goals of the convention or any clear prioritization of the objectives; nor was the subject of a work program debated and developed in any great detail, a point that we will return to briefly. Moreover, notwithstanding the signing of the convention, no determination has so far been made as to the size of a regular budget or the formula for quota allocations, although it is clear that the association will have to operate with quite limited resources.

Instead, much of the discussion centered on what often appeared to be topics of lesser importance and even questions of procedure. Precious time was lost as well; discussions bogged down with almost every imaginable aspect of the issue of the participation of France and the French Caribbean departments, a topic obviously irritating at times to certain delegations. Interestingly, direct participation of their Caribbean possessions was not an issue for the British and Dutch delegations, although it was made clear that these territories could not be authorized to sign the convention on their own behalf. As of the signing of the convention, much important business remained unfinished, which makes it difficult to offer any comprehensive assessment of the possible impact of the ACS.

The ACS Convention and Work Program

Purpose, Objectives, and Principles

The ACS Convention expresses in the first paragraph of its preamble a commitment to initiating "a new era characterized by the strengthening of cooperation and of cultural, economic, political, scientific, social, and technological relations" among the contracting states. In a subsequent paragraph, the parties indicate their preparedness to promote, consolidate, and strengthen the regional cooperation and integration process in the Caribbean region in order to create an enhanced economic space that will contribute to more competitive participation in international markets and more active and coordinated participation in various multilateral forums.

The association being created is conceived as "an organization for consultation, cooperation, and concerted action," according to Article III.1 of the convention. The article states further that the association's purpose is to identify and promote the implementation of policies and programs designed to:

1. Harness, utilize, and develop the collective capabilities of the Caribbean region to achieve sustained cultural, economic, social, scientific, and technological advancement;

2. Develop the potential of the Caribbean Sea through interaction among member states and with third parties;

3. Promote an enhanced economic space for trade and investment with opportunities for cooperation and concerted action, in order to increase the benefits which accrue to the peoples of the Caribbean from their resources and assets, including the Caribbean Sea; and

4. Establish, consolidate, and augment, as appropriate, institutional structures and cooperative arrangements responsive to the various cultural identities, developmental needs, and normative systems within the region.

Article III.2 of the ACS Convention specifies that in pursuit and fulfillment of these purposes, the association shall promote gradually and progressively among its members the following activities:

1. Economic integration, including the liberalization of trade, investment, transportation, and other related areas;

2. Discussion on matters of common interest for the purpose of facilitating active and coordinated participation by the region in various multilateral forums;

3. The formulation and implementation of policies and programs for functional cooperation;

4. The preservation of the environment and conservation of the natural resources of the region and especially of the Caribbean Sea;

5. The strengthening of friendly relationships among the governments and peoples of the Caribbean; and

6. Consultation, cooperation, and concerted action in such other areas as may be agreed upon.

Institutional Aspects

The structure of the ACS is uncomplicated. The permanent organs of the association are the ministerial council and the secretariat, with various special committees operating under the aegis of the former.

The ministerial council shall be the principal organ for policymaking and direction and will hold regular annual meetings at the headquarters of the association, without prejudice to the convening of special meetings as may be deemed necessary. Notwithstanding this status of the ministerial council, provision is also made for the holding of summit meetings on the proposal of any head of state or government of a member state after consultation with the rest or on the proposal of the ministerial council.

The council shall comprise such ministerial representatives and their alternates as each member state may consider appropriate. It is empowered to establish, initially on an ad hoc basis, the special committees that it considers necessary to assist in the performance of its functions. The convention creates specifically the following committees:

- The Committee on Trade Development and External Relations;
- The Committee for the Protection and Conservation of the Environment and of the Caribbean Sea;
- The Committee on Natural Resources;
- The Committee on Science, Technology, Health, Education, and Culture; and
- The Committee on Budget and Administration.

The secretariat, to be headed by a secretary-general, is intended to be lean and agile and to work in close coordination with the various subregional and regional bodies in carrying out its functions. As of this writing, no headquarters has been chosen, with the Dominican Republic, Trinidad and Tobago, and Venezuela in contention.[9]

The convention provides for the involvement of "social partners," defined as non-governmental organizations or other entities that are broadly representative of wide interests. Article IX (d) provides that the ministerial council recognize and accept the social partners and define their roles. It should be noted that the inclusion of the concept of social partners proved to be a difficult issue, less as a matter of principle than because certain delegations were concerned that this could open the floodgates for all types of organizations. The solution reached in effect allows for a case-by-case examination of eligibility for the right to participate in association deliberations.

The association will have three official languages: English, French, and Spanish. It will be financed through contributions by the member states to a regular budget approved on a biennial basis. In addition, a special fund will be established, with resources contributed on a voluntary basis by member states and by non-members or other entities, for the purpose of financing programs of technical cooperation and related research.

Work Program

Surprisingly little discussion took place at the technical level meetings about implementation of the objectives specified in the ACS Convention. As a result, certain delegations were unwilling to discuss possible budget quotas.[10] Yet some initial discussion did take place at the Caracas meeting concerning a possible two-year work program.

A document tabled at that meeting suggested that, aside from establishing the legal and administrative foundation to support the work of the ACS, the broad elements of the work program for the first two years might include the following:

1. The public relations function;
2. Information exchange and analysis;
3. Intra-ACS trade policy cooperation;
4. Intra-ACS investment facilitation;
5. Transport and communications;
6. Private sector linkages;
7. External economic relations;
8. Education and culture; and
9. Natural resources.[11]

The subject of a work program — together with the ACS budget, headquarters, secretary-general, and other matters — remains unresolved.

Six Areas of Challenge

In considering the nature of the task facing the association in the short to medium term, a number of challenges come readily to mind. In the remainder of this section, various aspects of six selected areas of challenge will be examined in order to demonstrate why they merit priority attention. In some cases, possible ways of tackling the challenges will be identified.

Defining Exclusive Space

An important task of the new organization will be to define its own operational space and to avoid duplication with the work of other regional institutions. This is particularly the case with joint coordination of economic positions on extra-ACS issues and in regard to third countries; the Latin American Economic System (Sistema Económico Latinoamericano — SELA) has so far had exclusive responsibility for such activities in Latin America and the Caribbean at large. The Rio Group also fulfills this function in a number of subject areas, particularly those of a more political character.

Yet it is conceivable that, for certain subjects, there could be a specificity about the Caribbean Basin's condition and interests that could be missed or become too diluted in negotiating consensus at the broader regional level. Consequently, these subjects merit special consideration within an ACS framework to buttress the group's position in broader regional discussions or in relation to nonregional actors. However, these issues would require careful identification. It is noteworthy that the one issue — NAFTA — that CARICOM leaders appear most hopeful that the ACS could influence through policy coordination is hardly susceptible to ACS coordination, since NAFTA signatory Mexico will also be part of the ACS membership. Indeed, Mexico is lukewarm about external policy coordination, which can make it a problematic area of activity within the new association.

On the other hand, the Caribbean Sea and related subject areas appear to constitute an activity cluster that would unquestionably fall within an ACS ambit, even though many specialized bodies deal with specific elements of the cluster. Here the ACS could perform the vitally important function of coordinating all related institutions under its umbrella. The same could be said in general terms for functional cooperation activities, which span a broad spectrum.

Specific Objectives

It is likely that, for most Caribbean Basin countries, the major drawing cards of the ACS have been prospects in the trade and investment areas. In particular, the idea of trade liberalization within such an enhanced space obviously could be an attractive proposition in the context of current moves to create a hemispheric free trade area. Currently, intra-ACS trade represents, for possibly all potential members, a very small share of their overall trade, especially if such exchanges with partners in the respective integration subgroups are excepted. However, the potential benefits of such relations have hardly been tapped and could be improved significantly if the ACS addresses, in addition to the issue of liberalization, related areas such as bridging the huge trade information gap and tackling the transportation problem.

Yet it must be recognized that there are also practical difficulties in developing an ACS-wide free trade area. Several questions need to be answered: how to coordinate the existing diversity of integration-related trade regimes involving the majority of the potential ACS member states and also how to forge an enhanced economic space from them. The potential membership belongs to the following integration bodies or trading arrangements: CARICOM, the Central American Integration System, the Andean Group (Colombia and Venezuela), the G-3, and NAFTA (Mexico), as well as other bilateral or plurilateral trading arrangements. One sticky point for CARICOM countries will be the extent of their willingness to move to reciprocal trading relationships with ACS partners.

Bringing about convergence among these subgroupings and arrangements within the Caribbean Basin will by no means be an easy task. Convergence within the ACS ambit may also be frustrated by competing processes that may prove even more attractive to some ACS members, for example, the possibility of a South American Free Trade Area as proposed by Brazil. Yet in many respects, the ACS is a microcosm of an eventual hemispheric free trade area, which may be problematic if solutions at the ACS level prove elusive. A flexible approach that allows progress among particular countries or groups — for example, CARICOM and Central American countries — instead of requiring uniform progress may provide the practical answer to this puzzle.

Membership Interaction

There is a general challenge to developing closer cooperation and integration across the entire spectrum of Caribbean Basin states. One aspect of this challenge relates to the way in which the kinship distribution of ACS membership will affect their interaction, with CARICOM member states making up twelve of the potential twenty-five ACS members, which coincides with voting power. Precisely because the CARICOM states are small, they may be inclined to operate as a bloc within the association. However, this would altogether complicate matters, because it could generate a similar response from the vast majority of the remaining ACS members, which are far more powerful in economic terms. Therein lies perhaps the greatest challenge in ACS decisionmaking.

At another level there exists as well the challenge of actively incorpo-rating non-independent associate members. The ACS Convention is almost unique in providing for the participation of this category of members, not merely with voice but also with vote, to the extent that they are constitutionally empowered. This provision accords with the spirit of the decision taken by CARICOM heads; it is also eminently sensible, if problems that know no borders in the Caribbean Basin, such as disease control, drug trafficking, environmental protection, maritime resource management, and disaster preparedness and response, are to be tackled successfully.

Yet implementing this decision will not be easy in every instance for cultural and practical reasons. CARICOM countries are long accustomed to a situation, for example, in which Montserrat, a non-independent territory, may participate in the integration process in all areas except foreign policy coordination. However, no such tradition exists within Latin America in bodies that are primarily political in nature.[12] This could cause problems even if non-independent territories are allowed real scope for participation by their metropoles; moreover, the determination of the extent of constitutional competence in certain areas may also be problematic.

Difficulties could easily arise as well with respect to participation of the French departments in particular. The CARICOM heads have aimed at active participation by the departments within the ACS,[13] and the departments expected as well to be granted some leeway in this respect. These hopes are likely to be thwarted by Paris, which has so far resisted allowing the overseas departments even the appearance of minimal autonomy in the preparatory meetings, clearly taking the lead in talks even while including representatives from the three departments on a unified French delegation, with resultant dissension within its ranks. It is vital, therefore, for ACS member states to anticipate ways in which such difficulties could arise if useful time is not to be lost on procedural questions, as has been the experience throughout the preparatory meetings.

Budgetary Aspects

All projections indicate that budgetary resources will be limited[14] and that the ACS secretariat will consequently be lean in staffing and have to collaborate closely with other regional and international institutions in both a technical and an organizational sense. There will also be a need to seek extra-budgetary financial support from international donors for certain program elements. Yet, the membership must avoid agreeing to too small a budget for the ACS to carry out its functions effectively.

The fact of the matter is that many of the smaller countries are unwilling to commit anything but the smallest quotas. The tiny Eastern Caribbean states belonging to the Organization of Eastern Caribbean States (OECS), a subgrouping of CARICOM, whose populations number less than one hundred thousand, are the extreme case. They now view the ACS largely in terms of compounding their burden of financing membership in CARICOM and the OECS and in other regional and international bodies. This situation has fueled some reluctance among the larger countries, notably Mexico, unwilling to bear the brunt of the ACS financial burden.

If too small a budget is eventually approved, a real danger exists that the association, apart from having to abandon its highly ambitious aspiration of making a so-called quantum leap in Caribbean development, will be hard-pressed even to develop feasible programs, and this would inevitably deprive the institution of vital political support.

Real Commitment

Although some potential ACS members have manifested interest in this undertaking and public statements of support for the initiative have been voiced in many capitals, a question still remains as to what degree real interest in the new association exists. Governments outside the ACS region, it should be noted, do not appear to have concerned themselves.

One does not sense that Caribbean Basin societies at large are enthused by the prospects of the new association or that there is much discussion taking place as to options and directions; on the contrary, one senses little interest or understanding of what might be involved. Indeed, even some of the CARICOM countries that initiated the ACS idea have subsequently demon-strated scant interest in the whole process leading to the creation of the ACS, as can be inferred from their absence in many of the preparatory meetings. This is particularly the case of the OECS countries, which do not anticipate that there will be much benefit for them in the new arrangement; they see their future tied principally to exports of services or traditional products to the North American or European markets. They are also concerned about extending their very limited human resources further in meeting obligations to the new body, including its budgetary implications.

For such reasons, the abiding impression is still that quite a few countries are joining the association, not because they are enthused by the idea and its possibilities, but because they find it preferable politically not to be left on the outside. Consequently, a major challenge to be faced, the solution to which will fall squarely on the shoulders of the first ACS executive and secretary-general, will be in finding ways of infusing the new body with a sense of excitement based on political relevance. This engendering of enthusiasm would have to occur during the early stages of the organization's existence and might only be accomplished through gaining support for an attractive work program.

Private Sector Role

Governments in the ACS region have time and again expressed their commitment to an increasing involvement of the private sector in cooperation activities. Today many governments routinely include private sector representation on national negotiation teams. For such reasons, some regionally organized private sector bodies, notably the Caribbean Association of Industry and Commerce, were particularly disappointed by the noninclusion of specific provisions in the ACS Convention for the active involvement of that sector.

The documentation before the meetings espoused the "real actor" concept, which it was argued normally refers to business and professional groups,[15] and the idea appeared to have support.[16] Yet in the view of this author, who was present at the negotiations, the present situation has come about, not because there was any opposition to the idea, but simply because the Caracas meeting did not get around to approving it because of severe time constraints. A private sector role was also contemplated in an earlier draft of the convention as part of an advisory board to be set up in order to assist the secretary-general,[17] but this idea was eventually excluded from the convention. While the provisional work program does make reference to the private sector, the elements considered in it are oriented toward encouraging and facilitating the development of linkages between chambers of commerce and the promotion of market surveys, business seminars, and trade visits. This is quite laudable, since systematized relationships among private sector organizations in the ACS region have failed to develop, but there is need to go further in promoting private sector/government interaction at the ACS level as well.

Indeed, it could be argued that an important opportunity was missed for institutionalizing private sector participation within the new organizational structure by not following the example of the MERCOSUR Industrial Council, which comprises representatives of the umbrella industrial organizations of the four member states (Argentina, Brazil, Paraguay, and Uruguay). Its aim is to evaluate the agreements being reached at the governmental level, to negotiate sectoral agreements, and to hold consultations on other integration process subjects. Yet an opportunity still exists for developing a meaningful government/private sector relationship within the ACS and, indeed, for collaboration between governments and other societal actors — if the social partner mechanism, which was previously explained, is used creatively. In the present regional and global context, this would appear to be an important prerequisite for successfully implementing several objectives of the ACS Convention.

Conclusion

The October 1992 decision of the heads of government of the Caribbean Community raised before Caribbean Basin governments and societies the proposition of an institutional framework for a collaborative purpose that was only very broadly defined, with the expectation that more precise purposes and objectives would eventually be specified. This, in a way, put the cart before the horse.

Such intergovernmental bodies are normally created only when the achievement of particular regional imperatives is clearly impossible or very difficult within the existing institutional apparatus or through bilateral and plurilateral action. The Organization of American States (OAS) was created because hemispheric security could not be specifically catered to otherwise. SELA catered on a permanent basis to the perceived imperative for developing countries of the Americas to coordinate external positions, and the promotion of cooperation in the economic and social fields was added. In the case of the ACS, it is less easy to demarcate the functional space that it is meant to fill exclusively and that has provided the imperative for its existence.

Yet the initiative managed to gain the requisite political support from governments in the Caribbean Basin, and the ACS Convention was signed within a relatively short time frame. This is all the more surprising amid the known reluctance on the part of most governments to contribute further to institutional proliferation and also in view of the difficulties many such organizations are currently encountering in staying afloat financially. Against this backdrop and owing to the fact that many substantial matters are still to be decided, the timetable for bringing this process to completion was arguably not only brief but also probably unrealistic. The ACS will undoubtedly face an uphill task from its very inception.

Ratification apart, in a very important sense the association is still not full-blown, and one would have to await decisions on the many items pending. The future of the ACS ultimately will depend on the degree to which its member states show genuine commitment to collaboration within the ACS framework. This commitment would itself depend on 1) the definition of a truly meaningful work program that would make collaboration attractive and fruitful within this ambit, and on 2) the provision of sufficient resources that could allow for effective implementation of objectives and generate internal and external confidence in the organization's future. The way in which the question of financial resources is eventually resolved will be decisive, but the propensity to create an institution "on the cheap" is alarmingly strong; many CARICOM countries initially were opposed to the idea of a permanent secretariat for cost reasons.

It is certainly difficult at this stage to make a judgment as to whether the association will be capable of an important impact in developmental terms on Caribbean Basin societies and interrelationships. An important prerequisite would be overcoming the challenges identified above. And it would be a considerable exaggeration to suggest that any feeling currently exists that the Caribbean Basin is poised for a new era because of the emergence of the ACS.

Editors' Note: At the first meeting of heads of state and government of the ACS held in Trinidad and Tobago on August 22-23, 1995, a Venezuelan, Simón Molina Duarte, was named as Secretary-General of the ACS. At the same meeting, Trinidad and Tobago was designated as the headquarters of the ACS Secretariat.

At the first ordinary ministerial council meeting held in Guatemala in November 1995, the ACS operating budget for its first fiscal year was established at US$1.5 million.

Notes

1. *Report of the Special Meeting of the Conference of Heads of Government, Trinidad and Tobago,* October 28-31, 1992.

2. The 1992 Protocol of Port of Spain, agreed to at the October special meeting, created the bureau of the CARICOM Heads of Government Conference, comprising three prime ministers on a rotation basis, assisted by the secretary-general of CARICOM. It was intended to act as an executive body with "competence to initiate proposals, update consensus, mobilize action, and secure implementation of CARICOM decisions."

3. *Summary of Conclusions of the First Meeting of the Bureau of the Conference of Heads of Government of the Caribbean Community,* December 15-16, 1992, Georgetown, Guyana, n.p., 6-13.

4. The October 1992 meeting considered that only Suriname, apart from some micro-territories like the Turks and Caicos Islands and the British Virgin Islands, was eligible for accession to CARICOM.

5. It was eventually decided that a final determination on this request should await the outcome of the West Indian Commission's recommendations.

6. See "Joint Communiqué CARICOM/Suriname/Group of Three Summit," *Caribbean Community Press Release 83/1993,* October 13, 1993.

7. Britain, France, the Netherlands, and the United States all have Caribbean possessions. The question had also been asked whether the State of Florida could participate in the initiative, in view of its economic importance to the Caribbean. *The Port of Spain Declaration on Trade and Investment* also speaks about broadening "the possibilities of systematic cooperation among the developing countries of the Caribbean Basin."

8. It should be noted that the CARICOM secretariat, acting on behalf of the Caribbean Community, played a lead role in the organization of meetings and preparation of documentation, up to the signing of the ACS Convention. It will be relied upon to perform these functions until a separate ACS secretariat is established.

9. Initially, Belize and Jamaica were also contenders, but they eventually gave their support to Trinidad and Tobago as the CARICOM candidate.

10. The Honduras delegation was quite explicit in stating that it would find it difficult to explain to the relevant minister the purpose of funds being committed.

11. Third Resumed Technical Meeting on the Establishment of an Association of Caribbean States, *Two-Year Work Programme for the Association of Caribbean States,* Attachment to TCH/ACS 94/3/2.

12. Account is taken here of the fact that within the UN-ECLAC system, the Caribbean Development and Cooperation Committee (CDCC) provides another example, but this is in essence a technical body.

13. The issue is obviously related to the fact that it would be politically inconvenient for Paris to participate when Washington cannot.

14. The upper-level figure considered so far is a mere US$2 million.

15. See Third Resumed Technical Meeting on the Establishment of the Association of Caribbean States, Caracas, June 27-28, 1994, The *"Real Actors," the "Social Partners," and the "Advisory Board" in the Association of Caribbean States*, TCH/ACS 94/3/4, June 20, 1994.

16. A Colombian draft of the convention, which was not made public, also included the real actor concept.

17. See *Working Document for the Technical Meeting on the Association of Caribbean States*, Kingston, Jamaica, March 16-18, 1994.

References

Caribbean Community. 1993. "Joint Communiqué CARICOM/Suriname/Group of Three Summit." Press Release 83/1933. October 13.

The "Real Actors," the "Social Partners," and the "Advisory Board" in the Association of Caribbean States. 1994. Third Resumed Technical Meeting on the Establishment of the Association of Caribbean States, June 27-18, 1994. TCH/ACS, 94/3/4. June 20.

Report of the Special Meeting of the Conference of Heads of Government, Trinidad and Tobago. October 28-31, 1992.

Summary of Conclusions of the First Meeting of the Bureau of the Conference of Heads of Government of the Caribbean Community. December 15-16, 1992. Georgetown, Guyana.

Two-Year Programme for the Association of Caribbean States. 1994. Third Resumed Technical Meeting on the Establishment of an Association of Caribbean States. Attachment to TCH/ACS, 94/3/2.

Working Document for the Technical Meeting on the Association of Caribbean States. March 16-18, 1994. Kingston, Jamaica.

Chapter Seven

Epilogue:
The Future Dynamics of
Caribbean-Latin American Relations

Anthony T. Bryan

From the fifteenth century, the Caribbean and Latin America have witnessed the brutal clash of European, African, and indigenous cultures in the processes of colonization and settlement. From the late nineteenth century and early twentieth century, in some Caribbean countries, such as Guyana and Trinidad, peoples from the Indian subcontinent have become a majority on the ethnic landscape. While the larger Latin American countries have been able to define their national and regional characteristics more precisely, starting in the early nineteenth century, the countries of the English-speaking Caribbean have had a longer association with Europe and only a more recent experience (since the 1960s) with political sovereignty, national identity, and efforts at regional integration.

Historically, both regions also have identified with the European- and with the North American-influenced world economy. Most Latin American nations have experienced a plethora of blatant or subtle interventions by the United States and European nations throughout their independent histories. The weaning of the English-speaking Caribbean countries away from Europe has been influenced by several factors, notably the political independence of the former British colonies, the geographic proximity to North America, a change in Caribbean migration patterns away from Europe and toward North America, U.S. investment and security interests in the Caribbean, the development of Caribbean tourism for the North American market, and the preeminence of the United States in media and telecommunications links in the region (Payne and Sutton 1992).

The English-speaking Caribbean response to safeguard traditional values has seen various attempts at formal West Indian integration. Beginning in 1975, the most notable of these, the Caribbean Community and Common Market (CARICOM), has emerged as one of the most successful examples of regional integration in the Western Hemisphere. Such success is measured not in terms of economic integration but rather by a record in functional cooperation and cultivation of acceptable political and regional values (Boxhill 1993, Samuel 1990). CARICOM also has provided the regional paradigm for economic development policy and foreign policy coordination in the English-speaking Caribbean. It has assumed a multifaceted character: a mechanism to reinforce a strong sense of kinship and cultural affinity, a pragmatic alliance in which economies of scale could benefit from a larger and more diverse pool of resources, and a flexible political coalition that reduces the disadvantages of very small size. Although CARICOM has the reputation of being almost an icon of English-speaking Caribbean unity, its hermetic quality is under challenge. Its membership is being widened, and its character is undergoing change (Bryan 1994a, 1994b, and 1995; West Indian Commission 1992).

Since the 1960s, and perhaps because of this moderately successful but very sentimental attachment to Commonwealth Caribbean integration, an insular developmental philosophy has come to characterize a region. Adapting to an integrating global economy has not been an easy task for its policymakers. The CARICOM countries find themselves faced with the dilemma of preserving the integrity of the movement, its cultural kinship, and its ethnic, racial, and linguistic identity, while trying to reconcile regional economic policies with global trends.

The Caribbean and Latin America today can be viewed in the context of the major contradiction that pervades world affairs, namely the simultaneous pressures toward centralization, globalization, and regional integration on the one hand and decentralization, fragmentation, and localizing tendencies on the other (Rosenau 1995a and 1995b). These broad conflicting international diplomatic, political, and economic trends pose challenges for both regions. Specifically, the genealogy of national and regional identities and characteristics prevailing up to the late 1980s is now under challenge from the new international landscape that began to emerge following the end of the Cold War and the dissolution of the communist bloc of nations (Braveboy-Wagner 1995, Serbin 1994b).

Dynamics of the Relationship

The dynamics of the Caribbean-Latin American relationship relate mostly to the interaction between the Commonwealth Caribbean and Latin America. While colonial political legacies and linguistic and ethnocultural circumstances have divided the Caribbean itself, as well as the Caribbean and Latin America, intraregional and interregional interaction between the peoples of the countries, mainly through migration for political or economic reasons, always has been part of the regional architecture. Informal networks of social and cultural contact provided by geographical proximity and migration — as in the case of Trinidad and Venezuela, or Jamaica and Cuba, or much of the former British West Indies with Panama and Central America — have been developed though perhaps not sustained (Lewis 1995, Serbin 1994a, Stone 1986).

In reality, academics and members of the political elite have been the principal promoters of closer Caribbean-Latin American links. Sometimes these same people also have been the major inhibitors of such interaction, depending on the political or racial climate of the times. Indeed, diplomatic relations (as in the case of the Belize-Guatemala and Venezuela-Guyana disputes, Trinidad and Tobago accession to membership in the Organization of American States in 1966, the Falkland Islands/Malvinas crisis in 1982, and the 1983 invasion of Grenada) often have fallen victim to distrust bred by the complex legacies of colonial division.

Moreover, during the 1960s, the relationship between Latin American states and the Commonwealth Caribbean countries was influenced mainly by geopolitical factors, including the latter's need for economic assistance, their use as a strategic buffer in Cold War security issues, and the mutual interest of both groups of countries in finding enhanced leverage in the North-South debate through the machinery of collective negotiation. Venezuela, Mexico, and Cuba traditionally demonstrated the greatest enthusiasm for bilateral ties to the countries of the Commonwealth Caribbean, while Brazil, Colombia, the Dominican Republic, and Haiti sought to strengthen their ties through functional arrangements.

During the 1970s and early 1980s, the activities of Venezuela, Mexico, and Cuba in particular helped to provide additional bargaining power and new policy options for the Commonwealth Caribbean states. Venezuela and Mexico derived their relative power within the region mostly from their vast petroleum resources and considerable financial weight in the hemisphere. The oil boom gave Venezuela the financial means to pursue a more aggressive foreign policy, including significant programs of foreign aid. Similarly, Mexico's petroleum wealth during the same period allowed it to project its own economic influence and political prestige as an alternative to both the United States and Cuba. Cuba's regional role — always projected as one of commitment to aid for progressive countries — demonstrated the ability of that country's leadership to perceive, test the limits of, and act within the available policy space in the Caribbean (Bryan 1990a).

In the 1990s, those dynamics have become more complex. As a result of major alterations in the global political economy, such as trade liberalization, subregional integration, and trading blocs, efforts at regional collaboration have intensified. Bilateral and multilateral initiatives for trade and commercial expansion, as well as movements toward subregional integration, have replaced the traditional geopolitical linkages. There is now a preeminence of economic issues over international political matters. Geo-economics has replaced geopolitics, and in both the Caribbean and Latin America, regional stability is now closely linked to economic rather than purely political interests.

In contrast to the earlier Cold War dynamic, the Commonwealth Caribbean-Latin American relationship is no longer restricted to specific elements of the governmental, economic, and intellectual elite. Today there is evidence of increasing relations at the level of political parties, convergence of diplomatic issues for private sector organizations and churches, of gender issues and ecological and environmental concerns (Serbin 1992 and 1994a). More important, the political directorates in both regions now strive to implement national policies that enhance economic development, show distributive justice, encourage the rule of law, protect fundamental human rights, and foster the growth of democratic institutions. Unfortunately, in many countries, concerns for alleviating poverty and income inequality caused by the reforms have not been integrated fully into proposals for economic growth. Many of the Caribbean's smaller economies are heavily dependent upon one (or a few) traditional export commodities for which world prices are not likely to rise. In many Caribbean and Latin American countries, increased crime, diminishing social support services, and dramatic increases in the poverty index, even in resource-rich countries (such as Venezuela and Trinidad and Tobago), constitute major negative impacts on the transition to free markets. The further impoverishment of the masses through the fiscal inability of governments to maintain essential social and infrastructural services is one of the new geo-economic realities (Bryan 1995).

The Future of Caribbean-Latin American Relations

Although it is difficult to assess future scenarios, the two areas that well might determine the future path of Commonwealth Caribbean-Latin American relations are trade and culture.

In Latin America and the Caribbean, the current momentum toward increased subregional integration and hemispheric trade follows the region's emergence from the so-called "lost decade" of the 1980s. The period was characterized by authoritarian regimes (mostly in Latin America) and by state-controlled industries and protected markets. However, even before the formation of the North American Free Trade Area (NAFTA), nearly every Latin American country began to construct agreements (either bilateral or multilateral) to promote trade by lowering tariffs and quotas. MERCOSUR, the Andean Pact, the Group of Three, and the Central American Integration System are the major subregional groupings that emerged. In the Caribbean region, CARICOM and now the wider grouping of the Association of Caribbean States (ACS) represent a similar evolution (Bryan 1984 and 1990b, Serbin 1991).

The NAFTA agreement among the United States, Canada, and Mexico established for all practical purposes the world's largest market, with an annual production capacity of US$7 trillion and a population of 377 million. According to NAFTA proponents, economic interaction among the three partners will be stimulated by reducing barriers to trade and investment while protecting intellectual property rights and the environment.

In Miami in December 1994, the leaders of 34 Western Hemisphere countries agreed on the formation of a Free Trade Area of the Americas (FTAA) by 2005, with concrete results to be made in completing negotiations toward this goal by the end of the century. The FTAA would make the Western Hemisphere the largest trading bloc in the world, with a combined gross domestic product (GDP) of more than US$7.7 trillion and a market of more than 745 million people. By comparison, the European Union (EU) has a combined GDP of US$7.2 trillion and a population of 370 million.

The Association of Caribbean States, with its headquarters in Port of Spain, Trinidad and Tobago, was established to develop closer relations between all Caribbean countries and the countries of northern South America, Central America, and Mexico. The ACS has the potential to become one of the largest blocs in the hemisphere, with a population of 220 million and combined GDP of some US$500 billion. The ACS is still in the organizational stage and has not yet declared itself a trade regime. It is too early to speculate on what role, if any, the ACS will play in the integration process. As two of the contributors to this volume have indicated, one must be sanguine about the expectations of any quantum leap in Caribbean-Latin American relations or the disappearance of linguistic, ethnocultural, or political barriers that have kept interaction between the two regions at a minimal level.

Integration into the global economy is the best option for CARICOM and Latin American countries. Preparations for hemispheric free trade should be seen as part of a process of erecting a framework to move them from the protected inward-looking arrangements of the past to a system that will improve their chances in dynamic global markets, in the Western Hemisphere, Western Europe, Asia, or elsewhere. CARICOM countries will find it difficult to meet the demands of the FTAA process, but trying to do so will lead toward meeting the criteria for global integration. The effort will include long-term strategic planning, market diversification, stronger institutional capacity, and efficient marketing. Managing the process will be more difficult for them than for larger Latin American countries. Many CARICOM members are more dependent on foreign trade for their fiscal revenues than are some of their larger Latin American neighbors. They also maintain a lower percentage of international reserves. Consequently, a strong dependence on external financing, a more liberalized trade system, and a concentrated and vulnerable export structure would pose greater external risks for them (Bryan 1996, McIntyre 1995, UN/ECLAC 1995). Relations with their Latin American neighbors should proceed apace, with the objective of encouraging investment and trade.

There are also other important points of concern in the context of the emerging hemispheric trading relationship. The current CARICOM goal of a single market and economy, and gradual progression to the FTAA by way of the ACS, might not be consistent necessarily with the pace of the Western Hemispheric movement. Latin American countries have demonstrated greater momentum than has the CARICOM group in extending their trading links and in moving toward the FTAA. The changes necessary within CARICOM, to prepare for, control, or benefit from the new hemispheric or global links, have been slow. The CARICOM single market and economy (CSM&E) is still evolving when, in fact, it was supposed to build momentum, via the ACS, to the hemispheric FTAA (UN/ECLAC 1995). Strengthening regional cooperation and formulating strategic alliances between CARICOM and the ACS, as a basis for developing production, increasing trade, and pursuing external negotiations, should proceed. The relationships often will be dictated by hard economic facts or sharp political realities, particularly as CARICOM moves toward closer trading relationships with other Caribbean island countries such as the Dominican Republic, Haiti, and Cuba. In any case, there are limits to which a CARICOM lobby can wield influence in a larger ACS grouping whose members have bloc and national interests of their own, and the Caribbean, however defined (CARICOM or ACS), is still a small, open, and vulnerable part of the world.

In this book, most of the authors have tried to confront the second factor in the future of the Caribbean-Latin American relationship, namely culture. While it is true that the reggae music of Jamaica and the calypso and soca music of Trinidad have traveled well and are widely rendered in Spanish and Portuguese by the Latin Americans, the dominant cultural models that have theoretically distinguished between the Caribbean and Latin America are under stress. They are not only being redefined by the changing roles of ethnicity, race, class, and gender in society but also by the new technologies. The cultural dynamics that still form the basis on which Caribbean and Latin American identities are defined are challenged by the diffusion of North American culture through the electronic highway and other newer communications technologies. Standardized and syncretic forms of mass culture are altering traditional forms of community and kinship relations almost in a virtual reality repeat of the earlier colonization process.

As geographical, political, and economic barriers disintegrate worldwide, the manner in which the Americas will be reconfigured is as yet an open question (Inotai 1994, Serbin 1994b). Can both regions retain their distinctive essence and their social imagery? Will geography and common historical legacies continue to define these two regions? Will ambivalent cultural identifications emerge that eventually can produce new cultural categories? Or will there be a new hemispheric cultural homogeneity — a vast new cultural American neighborhood (Ruprecht 1995)?

The various definitions of the Caribbean and Latin America that reflect multiple ethnohistorical, geographical, or regional variables, as implied in this book, may have limited relevance in the future. Generalizations about this mosaic of incredible complexity and diversity can, at minimum, leave some readers incandescent with skepticism and doubt and at best convey the impression that a great deal more research and policy implementation need to be attempted on this issue. In fact, the authors and editors wish to encourage the latter course because the genealogy of the wider Caribbean as a distinctive region in the Western Hemisphere, and as a region different from Latin America in particular, may be more complicated than either the dynamics of historical junctures or the interests of state actors in international economic relations suggest. The greatest task will be to forge into the consciousness of the peoples of the Caribbean and Latin America the imperative and the advantage of thinking and acting as one region, as the best and perhaps the only way to pursue and secure their respective aspirations. Perhaps in the future these distant cousins will contrive to negate the irreverent images of the Caribbean as "a set of islands with their backs to the sea" or of the mainland Latin American countries as "a group of islands surrounded by land."

References

Boxhill, Ian. 1993. *Ideology and Caribbean Integration*. Mona, Jamaica: University of the West Indies.

Braveboy-Wagner, Jacqueline. 1995. *Caribbean Diplomacy*. New York: The Caribbean Diaspora Press, Inc., of the City University of New York.

Bryan, Anthony T. 1996. "The Little Guys: Smaller Nations Want to go Global, but Cautiously." *Worldbusiness* 2 (2). March/April.

Bryan, Anthony T., ed. 1995. *The Caribbean: New Dynamics in Trade and Political Economy*. Coral Gables, Fla.: University of Miami North-South Center Press.

Bryan, Anthony T. 1994a. "The Caribbean Community in a Post-NAFTA World: Facing the Free Trade Dilemma. *North-South Focus* III (1).

Bryan, Anthony T. 1994b. "Más allá del tratado de libre comercio de América del Norte: el dilema de CARICOM." *Integración Latinoamericana* 19 (202): 35-42.

Bryan, Anthony T. 1990a. "The Latin American Geopolitical Environment: Trends and Influences on the Commonwealth Caribbean." In *Peace, Development and Security in the Caribbean: Perspectives to the Year 2000*, eds. A.T. Bryan, J. E. Greene, and T. Shaw. London: Macmillan Press/New York: St. Martin's Press, 85-101.

Bryan, Anthony T. 1990b. "The Integration Movement in Latin America: Theory, Process, Trends and Options," A.T. Bryan and Ludwik Dembinski, eds. Geneva, Switzerland: Graduate Institute of International Studies.

Bryan, Anthony T. 1984. "The CARICOM and Latin American Integration Experiences: Observations on Theoretical Origins and Comparative Performance." In *Ten Years of CARICOM*. Washington, D.C.: Inter-American Development Bank/ CARICOM, 71-94.

Inotai, Andras. 1994. "The New Regionalism and Latin America." In *The New Regionalism: Implications for Global Development and International Security*, eds. Bjorn Hettne and Andras Inotai. Helsinki, Finland: United Nations University, 1-49.

Lewis, David E. 1995. "The Latin Caribbean and Regional Cooperation: A Survey of Challenges and Opportunities." *Journal of Interamerican Studies and World Affairs* 37 (4): 25-55.

McIntyre, Arnold M. 1995. *Trade and Economic Development in Small Open Economies: The Case of the Caribbean Countries*. Westport, Conn., and London: Praeger Publishers.

Payne, Anthony J., and Paul K. Sutton. 1992. "The Commonwealth Caribbean in the New World Order: Between Europe and North America?" *Journal of Interamerican Studies and World Affairs* 34 (4) Winter: 39-75.

Rosenau, James N. 1995a. "Hurricanes are Not the Only Intruders: The Caribbean in an Era of Global Turbulence." mss. Conference on International Security in the Caribbean. Harvard University. October 20.

Rosenau, James N., and Mary Durfee. 1995b. *Thinking Theory Thoroughly: Coherent Approaches to an Incoherent World*. Boulder, Colo.: Westview Press.

Ruprecht, Alvina. 1995. "Latin America, the Caribbean and Canada: The New Cultural Neighbourhood." In *In the Hood: The Reordering of Culture in Latin America, the Caribbean and Canada*, eds. A. Ruprecht and C. Taiana. Ottawa, Canada: Carleton University Press, 3-12.

Samuel, Wendell. 1990. "Regional Cooperation as an Element of Caribbean Development Strategy." In *Integration and Participatory Development*, ed. Judith Wedderburn. Kingston, Jamaica: Friederich Ebert Stiftung, 7-79.

Serbin, Andrés. 1991. "The CARICOM States and the Group of Three: A New Partnership Between Latin American and the Non-Hispanic Caribbean?" *Journal of Interamerican Studies and World Affairs* 33 (2) Summer: 53-80.

Serbin, Andrés. 1992. *Medio ambiente, seguridad y cooperación regional en el Caribe*. Caracas, Venezuela: Editorial Nueva Sociedad.

Serbin, Andrés. 1994a. "Transnational Relations and Regionalism in the Caribbean." In *Trends in U.S.-Caribbean Relations. The Annals of the American Academy of Political and Social Science* 533, May: 139-150.

Serbin, Andrés. 1994b. "Reconfiguraciones geoeconómicas y transiciones políticas en el Caribe de los noventa." In *El Caribe y Cuba en la Posguerra Fria*, eds. Andrés Serbin and Joseph Tulchin. Caracas, Venezuela: Editorial Nueva Sociedad, 11-25.

Stone, Carl. 1986. *Power in the Caribbean Basin: A Comparative Study of Political Economy*. Philadelphia: Institute for the Study of Human Issues.

United Nations Commission for Latin America and the Caribbean (UN/ECLAC). 1995. *Integration and Caribbean Development: Reconciling Regional Policies with Global Trends*. LC/CAR/G 464. December.

West Indian Commission. 1992. *A Time for Action: The Report of the West Indian Commission*. Black Rock, Barbados: West Indian Commission.

Index

A

ACE (Association of Caribbean Economists) 5, 7, 97
ACP (African, Caribbean and Pacific Countries) 29
ACS (Association of Caribbean States) 6, 8, 11, 78, 79, 83, 86, 87, 88, 90, 91, 92, 93, 97, 98, 99, 100, 101, 102, 103, 104, 105, 106, 108, 109, 110, 111, 112, 113, 114, 115, 122, 123, 124
membership in 97, 103, 109, 110
structure of 107
ACS Convention 106, 108, 111, 113, 114
African, Caribbean and Pacific Countries. *See ACP*
Afro-Antilleanism 55, 60, 61, 64
ALADI (Latin American Integration Association) 9
Alexis, Jacques Stephen 61
Andean Group 5, 110
Andean Pact 100, 101, 102, 122
Arciniegas, Germán 57
Asociación Latinoamericana de Integración. *See ALADI*
Association of Caribbean Economists. *See ACE*
Association of Caribbean States. *See ACS*

B

black legend 56
black power 19, 41, 42, 43, 44, 46
Brathwaite, Edward K. 60, 65, 67

C

CACM (Central American Common Market) 5

CAFRA (Caribbean Association for Feminist Research and Action) 7
calypso 124
Carew, Jan 56, 68, 70
Caribbean Association for Feminist Research and Action. *See CAFRA*
Caribbean Basin 5, 6, 8, 9, 10, 11, 83, 97, 98, 99, 100, 103, 104, 109, 110, 111, 112, 114, 115
countries 6, 8, 9, 10, 11, 78, 90, 92, 97, 99, 103, 104, 109
Caribbean Community. *See Caribbean Community and Common Market*
Caribbean Community and Common Market. *See CARICOM*
Caribbean Conservationist Association 7
Caribbean Development and Cooperation Committee. *See CDCC*
Caribbean Development Bank. *See CDB*
Caribbean Free Trade Area. *See CARIFTA*
Caribbean Studies Association. *See CSA*
Caribbean Universities and Research Institutes. *See UNICA*
Caribbeanism 61
CARICOM (Caribbean Community and Common Market) 4, 5, 6, 10, 29, 79, 80, 81, 82, 83, 84, 85, 86, 87, 88, 90, 91, 92, 93, 98, 99, 100, 101, 102, 103, 104, 105, 109, 110, 111, 112, 119, 120, 122, 123, 124
collaboration with OAS 88, 89
countries in 9, 10, 11, 45, 100, 102, 105, 110, 111, 112, 114, 120, 123
formation of 90
intra-CARICOM coordination 88

Production
Notes

This book was printed on 60 lb. Glatfelter, Natural, text stock with a 10 point CIS cover stock.

The text and index of this volume, designed by Susan Kay Holler, were set in Garamond at the North-South Center Press, using Aldus PageMaker 4.2, on a Power Macintosh 8500/120 computer.

The cover was created by Mary M. Mapes using Adobe Illustrator 5.0 for the design and QuarkXpress 3.1 for the composition and color separation.

The book was edited by Jayne M. Weisblatt, Kathleen A. Hamman, and Mary E. D'León.

This publication was printed by Thomson-Shore, Inc. of Dexter, Michigan.